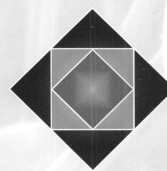

John Mills &
Peter Evans

# Core
# Chemistry

CAMBRIDGE
UNIVERSITY PRESS

| | |
|---|---|
| **Series editor** | Bryan Milner |
| | Jean Martin |
| | John Mills |
| **Chemistry author** | John Mills |
| ***Core Science* authors** | Jenifer Burden |
| | Paul Butler |
| | Zoë Crompton |
| | Sam Ellis |
| | Peter Evans |
| | Jean Martin |
| | Bryan Milner |
| **Consultants** | Kate Chaytor |
| | Nigel Heslop |
| | Martyn Keeley |

PUBLISHED BY THE PRESS SYNDICATE OF THE UNIVERSITY OF CAMBRIDGE
The Pitt Building, Trumpington Street, Cambridge, United Kingdom

CAMBRIDGE UNIVERSITY PRESS
The Edinburgh Building, Cambridge CB2 2RU, United Kingdom
40 West 20th Street, New York, NY 10011-4211, USA
477 Williamstown Road, Port Melbourne, VIC 3207, Australia
Ruiz de Alarcón 13, 28014 Madrid, Spain
Dock House, The Waterfront, Cape Town 8001, South Africa

http://www.cambridge.org

© Cambridge University Press 1999

First published 1999
Reprinted 2001, 2002

Printed in the United Kingdom at the University Press, Cambridge

*Typeface* Stone Informal 11/14 pt, 10.5/14 pt, 10/13 pt

*A catalogue record for this book is available from the British Library*

ISBN 0 521 66638 4 paperback

Designed and produced by Gecko Ltd, Bicester, Oxon

Cover photo: Velcro Eye of Science/Science Photo Library

# Contents

# How this book is organised

*Core Chemistry* is designed to cover the chemistry (AT3) component of the National Curriculum for Science at Key Stage 3. It also covers the chemistry requirement of the Common Entrance Examination at 13+.

For most pupils, Key Stage 3 comprises the first three years (Years 7, 8 and 9) of their secondary education, culminating in the Key Stage 3 SATs towards the end of Year 9.

If these pupils are to do themselves justice in the SATs tests, they really need to have made significant, recent use of all the scientific ideas that they might encounter in the SATs.

To ensure that this happens, the content of *Core Chemistry* is organised as follows.

| BASIC CONCEPTS [for all pupils, normally in Years 7 and 8] | CONSOLIDATION [for all pupils, normally in Year 9] | + DEVELOPMENT [for some pupils, normally in Year 9] |
|---|---|---|
| This section of the book: | This section of the book: | These additional (Core+) pages, at the end of each topic in the Consolidation section: |
| ■ covers the great majority of concepts needed for KS3 SATs up to Level 6; | ■ revisits all the Basic Concepts, in different contexts and at a quicker pace; | ■ extend basic concepts further and/or apply them to more difficult contexts; |
| ■ introduces new ideas gently, one at a time, with ample opportunity for pupils to confirm their mastery of each new idea immediately after it is introduced. | ■ extends them, where necessary, so that pupils are fully prepared for KS3 SATs up to Level 6. | ■ prepare pupils for KS3 SATs up to Level 7. |

Pages 8 and 9 are set out so that they show where each concept area in the Basic Concepts section is Consolidated and further Developed.

It shows, for example, that:

| Basic concepts about matter are covered in: | The basic concepts are consolidated and extended a little in: | The ideas are further developed and applied to other contexts in: |
|---|---|---|
| 1.2 Solid, liquid and gas<br>1.3 Explaining the way things are | C1.3 Solids, liquids and gases<br>C1.4 Making models of matter | C1.10 Density of gases<br>C1.11 What makes a solid melt?<br>C1.12 Why do liquids evaporate? |

The links between the different sections are shown at the top of the relevant pages of the book.

It should be noted that *Core Chemistry* does <u>not</u> attempt to cover the additional content that may be required for the SATs Extension papers. The additional material needed to answer some of the questions in these papers derives from part of the Programme of Study specified by the National Curriculum for Key Stage 4. Teachers who feel that their pupils are ready for this material in Year 9 are advised to use the relevant parts of textbooks written to support Key Stage 4.

## ■ Pupils' notes

The text is liberally sprinkled with questions designed to provide pupil interaction and allow them to confirm their mastery of ideas as they are presented. The outcomes of these questions are <u>not</u> intended to result in a coherent set of notes for revision – this is the purpose of the summary sections (see below).

Some of these questions have a magnifier symbol printed alongside. This indicates that the answer to the question <u>cannot</u> be found in the text. Pupils are expected to find out the answer from elsewhere.

A 'working notebook' for answering text questions is recommended. This notebook might also be used for any other written work which is not intended to form a permanent record for revision purposes, such as some aspects of practical work, answers to questions from Question banks in the *Supplementary Materials*, etc.

The key words in each spread are highlighted in **bold**. Pupils use these words to complete the summary sections headed *What you need to remember* (WYNTR). The accumulated set of WYNTR passages comprises a record of the knowledge and understanding that pupils will need for SATs.

A separate notebook for WYNTR summaries is recommended. This will make a useful reference for revision.

Since they are to be used for revision, it is, of course, essential that pupils' completed summaries are correct. These are supplied at the back of *Core Chemistry* and can be used for checking.

## ■ Practical work

The content and presentation of any particular piece of practical work will depend on what the teacher considers are the main aims of that practical assignment, e.g. to make otherwise abstract ideas more concrete and meaningful or to develop and assess Sc1 skills and abilities. Consequently, practical work on a particular topic may vary considerably. So, though *Core Chemistry* helps to develop Sc1 skills and abilities by presenting information about investigations for pupils to interpret and evaluate, detailed instructions for pupils' practical work are <u>not</u> provided. It is assumed that the teacher will provide the practical work to support topics that best suits the needs of their pupils.

The text of *Core Chemistry* has also been presented in a way that does not depend on practical work; it is completely stand-alone.

## ■ Supplementary materials

*Core Chemistry Supplementary Materials* are available to support the pupils' text. This fully photocopiable resource assists teaching and lesson-planning by providing practical suggestions, tests, worksheets (for homework or class use) and answers to all the questions in the pupils' text. There is also a matching grid to show how *Core Chemistry* covers the Key Stage 3 Science National Curriculum.

These materials comprise:

- a *Commentary* for each double-page spread of the pupils' text which includes:
  - full details of the expected *Outcomes to questions* in the text, written in language that pupils themselves are expected to use;
  - *Suggestions for practical activities*;
- *Worksheets* wherever these are particularly useful;
- *Topic tests* and *Question banks*.

## The Common Entrance Examination at 13+

Pupils preparing for the Common Entrance Examination at 13+ will need to have covered the material in *Core Chemistry* a year earlier than pupils preparing for SATs.

This can be achieved via several different approaches:

- embarking on *Core Chemistry* a year earlier (e.g. in the preparatory school sector);
- covering the Basic Concepts section in a single year and proceeding to the Consolidation and Development section the following year;
- visiting each topic area <u>once only</u> in a two-year programme, i.e. covering the Consolidation and Development section immediately after the relevant Basic Concepts section. When using this strategy, only selected aspects of the Consolidation material may be needed and the remainder omitted.

# Ways through this book

The word 'CORE+' appears at the top of the Development pages as a reminder that they are needed only for the higher-tier Key Stage 3 SATs.

# 1.1 The right one for the job

Things like how strong a material is, or if heat passes through it, are called its **properties**. We choose a material for a particular job because it has the right properties for that job.

## ■ Why use stainless steel for a pan?

Stainless steel is good for making pans.

1  Write down <u>three</u> properties of stainless steel that make it good for this job. Give a reason for each property you choose.

The handle must not get hot.

Heat must go through the pan.

plastic handle

thick base spreads the heat

| Properties of stainless steel |
| --- |
| shiny polished surface |
| does not rust |
| hard wearing |
| not too heavy |
| does not melt easily |
| does not catch fire |
| nice to look at |
| heat passes through it |

## ■ Properties of wood

Wood is used for doors. You can cut and shape wood easily. It is strong.

2  Write down <u>three</u> properties of wood that make it good for doors.

3  Write down <u>two</u> properties of wood that explain why it is not used to make cooking pans. (Hint. Look back at the table of properties of stainless steel.)

We usually talk about 'heat', but the correct technical term is 'thermal energy'.

Wood can be cut to fit the frame.

Holes can be cut for the letterbox and locks.

Wood is a poor conductor of heat. (It stops heat going in and out.)

## ■ Materials we can see through

We need to see through a window. So we make a window out of a **transparent** material.

**4** Write down <u>three</u> other important properties for a window. Give a reason for each.

**5** Why is glass better than clear plastic for the windows in a house?

**6** Why is plastic better than glass for the windows in a child's play house?

Glass is transparent (it lets light through).

Glass keeps wind and rain out.

Glass does not dissolve in rain.

Glass does not scratch or mark as easily as plastic.

If glass breaks, the pieces are very sharp.

## ■ Conductors and insulators of electricity

Materials that let electricity flow through them easily are called **conductors**. All metals conduct electricity.

Materials called **insulators** do not let electricity flow through.

**7** Copy and complete the sentences.

The case of a plug is made of _____ because it is an _____.

The pins of a plug are made of _____ because it is a _____.

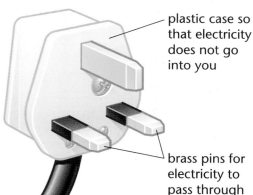

plastic case so that electricity does not go into you

brass pins for electricity to pass through

---

**WHAT YOU NEED TO REMEMBER** (Copy and complete using the **key words**)

**The right one for the job**

The things that make a material good for a particular job, like how hard it is, are called its _____.

Materials you can see through are _____.

All metals let electricity pass through them. They are called _____.
Materials that do not let electricity through are called _____.

**Note:** You must be able to say what properties other materials must have to make them good for various jobs.

**More about materials: C1.1**

# 1.2 Solid, liquid and gas

Some things are solid, some things are liquid and some things are gas. Solids, liquids and gases have different properties.

For example, gases and liquids will **flow**. Solids do not flow.

1 Water and gas come into people's houses through pipes. Why can they be delivered this way?

2 Look at the pictures. Explain why Sadia cannot pour the milk.

3 Copy and complete the table using the following substances. (They are all shown in the picture.)

snow, glass, pottery, orange juice, plastic, water, steam, steel, wood

| Solid | Liquid | Gas |
| --- | --- | --- |
|  |  |  |

## ■ Liquids change shape, gases fill space, solids stay the same

Liquids **change** shape to fit what they are in. Lumps of solid keep the same **shape**. A gas will spread out to fill any **space**.

4 Answer the questions. For each question write down why you think the substance is a solid, liquid or gas.

(a) What does the brown substance do when the plate is removed?

(b) What happens to the shape of the meths when the bottle is tilted?

(c) What happens to the shape of the ice cube when the board is tilted?

On a snowy day Sadia gets her milk from the doorstep.

It is cold and the top of the milk is frozen solid.

Sadia cannot pour the milk because the top is frozen.

(a)
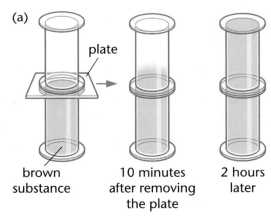

plate

| brown substance | 10 minutes after removing the plate | 2 hours later |

(b)
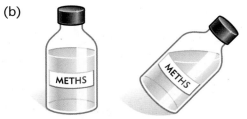

(c)    ice cube

## ■ Some substances are heavier than others

The table shows how heavy different substances are. To make the table fair, the figures are for one cubic centimetre of each substance. One cubic centimetre is about the size of a small dice.

Solids and liquids are heavier than gases. We say that solids and liquids are **denser** than gases.

| Mass of one cubic centimetre. | | |
|---|---|---|
| Solid | Liquid | Gas |
| iron 7 g | water 1 g | air 0.0013 g |
| gold 18 g | olive oil 0.9 g | steam 0.0006 g |
| pine 0.5 g | petrol 0.9 g | |
| cork 0.2 g | Ribena 1.3 g | |

5 Which solids are denser than water?

6 Which solids are less dense than water?

7 How many times more dense is:

   **(a)** iron than water?

   **(b)** water than cork?

## ■ Floating and sinking

Cork floats on water because it is a **less dense** substance than water. A lump of iron **sinks** in water because it is a denser substance than water.

8 Look at the table again. Which solids will float on water?

9 Copy the diagram of oil and water.

Underneath the diagram, copy and complete this sentence.

The oil floats on the water because it is less _____ than the water.

*A suitcase full of air is a lot lighter than one full of gold!*

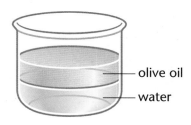

olive oil
water

---

### WHAT YOU NEED TO REMEMBER (Copy and complete using the **key words**)

**Solid, liquid and gas**

Solids have their own _____. Liquids and gases can _____ shape. A gas spreads out to fill any _____.

Gases and liquids will _____ through pipes.

Solids and liquids are heavier substances than gases; we say they are _____.

Something floats on a liquid if it is _____ _____ than the liquid. A lump of iron _____ in water because it is a denser substance than water.

**More about solids, liquids and gases: C1.3**

# 1.3 Explaining the way things are

A lot of cars have airbags in them. An airbag can save a driver in a crash.

When the bag fills with air, it makes a cushion. This stops the driver hitting the wheel. Air works because it is a gas. You can squash a gas and it will spring back.

Look at the pictures.

1 (a) What happens to the air in the tube when the weight is put on the top?

   (b) What happens to the air in the tube when the weight is taken away?

2 What happens when you do the same test with a tube of liquid?

3 What happens when you do the same test with a block of solid?

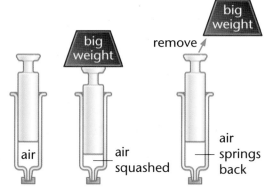

*Air squashes and springs back.*

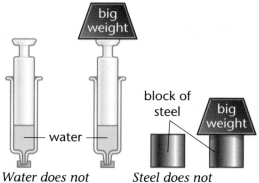

*Water does not squash.*    *Steel does not squash.*

## ■ Why can a gas be squashed?

Gases are made up of tiny **particles** that **move** about at high speed.

The particles are **far apart**. They do not hold each other together.

4 What is a gas made up of?

5 What do gas particles do when they hit each other?

6 Why can you squash (compress) a gas?

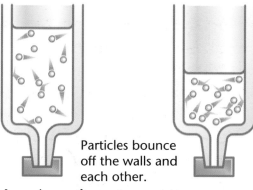

Particles bounce off the walls and each other.

*A gas is mostly empty space, so you can squeeze the particles into a smaller space.*

■ **How are the particles arranged in a liquid?**

The particles are very close together in a liquid. There is not very much space between the particles.

Though the particles in a liquid stay close together they are always moving about. They **change places** with each other all the time.

7  Why is it hard to squash (compress) a liquid?

8  You can pour a liquid into a container with a different shape. Explain why you can do this.

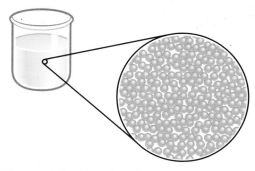

*The particles in a liquid move around each other. There is no pattern.*

*You can **pour** a liquid.*

■ **What about solids?**

The particles in a solid hold each other together **strongly**. They are packed **close together**.

The particles can jiggle about or **vibrate**, but they do not change places.

Particles in a solid are usually fixed in a pattern.

9  How are the particles arranged in a solid?

10  Why is it hard to squash a solid?

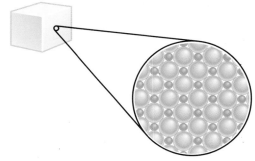

*Particles in a solid are fixed in a pattern.*

**WHAT YOU NEED TO REMEMBER** (Copy and complete using the **key words**)

**Explaining the way things are**

Solids, liquids and gases are all made of _____.

In solids, the particles hold each other together _____. They cannot change places, but they can _____.

In liquids, the particles stay close together but they can _____ _____ with each other. This means you can _____ a liquid.

In a gas there is a lot of space between the particles. The particles _____ around at high speed.

You can squash a gas because the particles are _____ _____.
It is hard to squash a liquid or a solid because the particles are _____ _____.

**More about models of matter: C1.4**

# 1.4 Mixing solids and liquids

To make drinks sweet you add sugar. When you add sugar to water and stir for a time you can't see the sugar any more. But it is still there in the water. The sugar <u>dissolves</u> in the water and produces a **solution**.

1 Write down <u>four</u> solids which dissolve in water and are commonly used in the kitchen.

*Just mix with water …*

### ■ Making solutions sweeter

Vicky added spoonfuls of sugar to two beakers of water. She stirred the water 10 times after adding each spoonful to see if all the sugar would dissolve.

Look at the diagram of the experiment.

2 Why can beaker B dissolve more sugar than beaker A?

3 Write down how this investigation was made fair.

More sugar dissolves in **hot** water than cold. The sugar is more <u>soluble</u> in hot water.

4 How could you dissolve more spoonfuls of sugar in the water in beaker A?

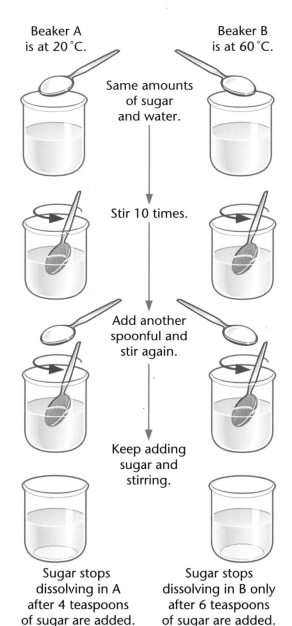

Beaker A is at 20 °C.    Beaker B is at 60 °C.

Same amounts of sugar and water.

Stir 10 times.

Add another spoonful and stir again.

Keep adding sugar and stirring.

Sugar stops dissolving in A after 4 teaspoons of sugar are added.

Sugar stops dissolving in B only after 6 teaspoons of sugar are added.

## ■ Cleaning the mess!

Graffiti on desks or a wall is a nuisance. Water will not always clean the coloured dye from ink or marker pens. To remove graffiti we need a liquid which dissolves the dye. This liquid is called a **solvent**.

5 **(a)** Which liquid removes the dye in the picture?

**(b)** Does the dye dissolve in water?

**(c)** Which liquid is a good solvent for dye?

The dye which dissolves in the solvent is called the **solute**.

6 Copy the table of words. Then copy the correct definition next to each word.

| Word | Definition |
|------|-----------|
| dissolve | |
| solvent | |
| solution | |
| solute | |

*Definitions*

■ The name for a substance which dissolves in a liquid.

■ A liquid which contains a dissolved substance.

■ A liquid in which another substance will dissolve.

■ This is what happens when a solid, liquid or gas disappears into a liquid.

 Coca Cola is a solution. Find out the solvent and main solutes in Coca Cola.

**WHAT YOU NEED TO REMEMBER** (Copy and complete using the **key words**)

**Mixing solids and liquids**

When a substance dissolves in a liquid we get a _____.

Substances often dissolve better when the liquid is _____.

The liquid that the substance goes into is called the _____. The dissolved substance is called the _____.

More about mixtures: C1.6

# 1.5 Melting and boiling

Many solids melt when they are heated. They change into a liquid. This happens at a temperature called its **melting point**.

If you make a liquid hot enough, it will boil. The temperature at which this happens is called its **boiling point**. As a liquid boils it changes into a **gas**.

## ■ Comparing melting points and boiling points

The table shows temperatures of melting and boiling for some substances.

For each substance, the temperature of the boiling point is always **higher** than that of the melting point.

1  Which substances in the table are solids at 20°C?

2  Which substance in the table is a liquid at 20°C?

3  Why do you need a very hot furnace to turn iron metal into a liquid?

4  Which other substance in the table is a metal?

## ■ Making ice lollies

To change a liquid to a solid you must cool it down to below its melting point. So to change water to ice you must cool it to below 0°C.

Arthur tried to make ice lollies. He put one lolly tray into the main part of the fridge. He put the other tray into the freezer section.

5  Which tray will contain the best lollies after a day? Explain your answer.

6  To get the lollies out of the tray, Arthur put the tray in hot water for a few seconds.
Explain why this works.

We measure temperatures in degrees Celsius (°C).

aluminium metal    sulphur    iron metal

water

*All these substances are at room temperature (20°C).*

Metals usually have higher melting points and boiling points than substances that are not metals.

| Substance | Melting point (°C) | Boiling point (°C) |
|---|---|---|
| aluminium | 666 | 2470 |
| water | 0 | 100 |
| iron | 1535 | 2750 |
| sulphur | 113 | 445 |

fridge at 2°C

freezer at −18°C

## Making the tea

Arthur was disappointed with his efforts to make lollies. He decided to help with the tea instead. He heated water in a kettle and very quickly the water turned into steam.

Arthur noticed that as the steam reached the kitchen window it turned back into water (we say that the water <u>condensed</u>). The water began streaming down the glass.

**7** What happens to the steam when it hits the window?

**8** Why do you notice this more on a cold day?

## Different boiling points

A test tube of alcohol was put into a beaker of very hot water. The alcohol in the test tube started to boil even though the water was not boiling!

water at 90 °C

alcohol boiling

**9** Why is the alcohol boiling even though the water is not boiling?

To check what liquids are, scientists often measure their boiling point. A pure liquid always boils at the same temperature.

| Substance | Boiling point (°C) |
|-----------|--------------------|
| alcohol   | 78                 |
| water     | 100                |

**10** Look at the diagrams.

(a) Which liquid is water?

(b) Which liquid is alcohol?

(c) Which liquid might be paraffin?

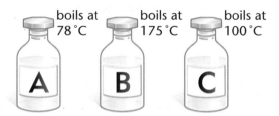

boils at 78°C

boils at 175°C

boils at 100°C

A  B  C

**WHAT YOU NEED TO REMEMBER** (Copy and complete using the **key words**)

**Melting and boiling**

Many solids have a temperature at which they will melt. This is called the _____ _____ of the solid.

The temperature at which a liquid boils is called the _____ _____. As a liquid boils, it changes into a _____.

Boiling point temperatures are always _____ than melting point temperatures.

**More about warmer and colder: C1.5**

# 1.6 Heat in, heat out

**REMEMBER** from page 18

The melting point of ice is 0 °C.

## Heating things doesn't always make them hotter

When you heat things they usually become hotter. But this does not always happen.

Look at the diagrams.

1 What happens to the water when you first start heating it?

2 What is the temperature of the water when it starts to boil?

3 What happens to the temperature of the boiling water when you keep on heating it?

The beaker is being heated as the water boils but the temperature is staying the same.
**Energy** from the hot flame makes the water change into a gas.

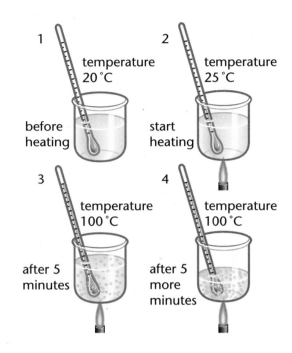

1 temperature 20 °C — before heating

2 temperature 25 °C — start heating

3 temperature 100 °C — after 5 minutes

4 temperature 100 °C — after 5 more minutes

## Melting ice

For an ice cube to melt it must take in energy. It takes this energy from the air or the dish it is on. To make the ice melt we have to make it hotter, so we have to **transfer** energy to the ice from its surroundings. This makes the surroundings colder.

4 For each of the ice cubes in the picture, say whether it would melt, and give a reason for your answer.

5 Which cube, A or B, would take the longest to melt? Explain your answer.

ice cube A
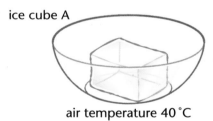
air temperature 40 °C

ice cube B
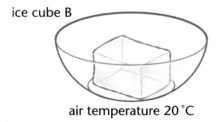
air temperature 20 °C

ice cube C
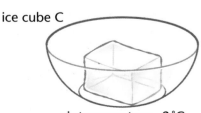
air temperature −2 °C

## ■ Getting rid of water

Anne left a measuring cylinder of water on a balance for a week.

**6** Give <u>two</u> things that have changed about the water in one week.

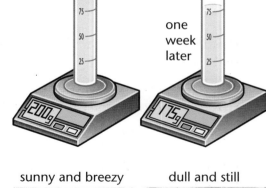

one week later

The water that has gone has changed into a gas. We call this change **evaporation**.

You can make evaporation happen more quickly by **heating** things.

You can make evaporation happen more quickly by **blowing** on the liquid surface.

sunny and breezy    dull and still

**7** Give <u>two</u> ways that a hair dryer helps water evaporate from your hair.

**8** Which set of washing will dry quickest? Give <u>two</u> reasons for your answer.

## ■ Cooling things down

Water evaporates from wet things. This makes these things a bit **colder**.

**9** Look at the pictures. Which person will feel coolest? Give a reason for your answer.

**10** How does sweating help you cool down?

air temperature 20 °C

dry person

person soaked in water at 20 °C

---

**WHAT YOU NEED TO REMEMBER** (Copy and complete using the **key words**)

**Heat in, heat out**

When we boil a liquid, we give _____ to the liquid.

When an ice cube is melted we _____ heat to the ice.

The change from liquid to gas is called _____.

We can make evaporation happen more quickly by _____ the liquid, and by _____ on the liquid surface.

Evaporation makes things get _____.

**More about warmer and colder: C1.5**

# 1.7 Other effects of heating and cooling

Heating things can change them from solid to liquid or from liquid to gas. Cooling things can do the opposite.

Heating and cooling can also change things in other ways.

## How long is a piece of metal?

It depends on the temperature! If a bar of metal gets hot it will **expand**; this means it gets longer. If the metal cools down it will **contract**; this means it gets shorter.

1  Which picture shows telephone wires in summer?

2  Which picture shows telephone wires in winter?

## Damaging heat

Many other substances expand when they get hot – not just metals.

If a substance can't expand when it gets hot, **push** forces are produced. If a substance can't contract as it cools, **pull** forces are produced. These forces can do lots of damage.

3  Copy this table. Complete it using the information in the pictures.

| Example | Damage caused by contraction or expansion | How damage is prevented |
|---|---|---|
| telephone wires | | |
| runway | | |

4  (a)  What is the expanding concrete on the runway pushing against?

   (b)  Why does the bitumen stop the concrete cracking?

A

Telephone wires go slack when they get hot and expand.

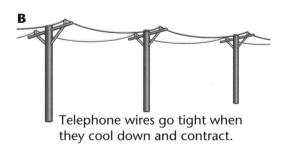

B

Telephone wires go tight when they cool down and contract.

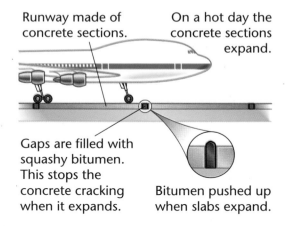

Runway made of concrete sections.

On a hot day the concrete sections expand.

Gaps are filled with squashy bitumen. This stops the concrete cracking when it expands.

Bitumen pushed up when slabs expand.

*Telephone wires are put up so they are slack. If they contract in cold weather they get tighter but do not snap.*

## Expanding and contracting liquid

Like solids, liquids expand or contract when they get hot or cool down.

Mercury is a liquid metal found in many types of thermometer.

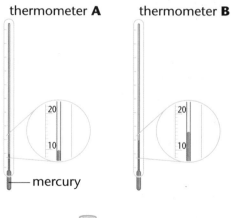

5 Write down the readings on both thermometers.

6 Describe what happens to the length of mercury in the thermometer when the temperature falls.

7 Does the mercury expand or contract when the temperature falls?

8 Wine bottles always have a gap at the top of the liquid inside the bottle. Explain why.

 Find out the melting point and boiling point of mercury and alcohol (ethanol). Why do you think ethanol is sometimes used in thermometers to replace mercury?

The force of an expanding liquid will push out the cork. Air is squashy so it makes room for the wine to expand.

## Gases getting hot

Inside the wine bottle there is no room for the air to expand.
But air will expand when it is heated if there is nothing to stop it.

9 Explain what happens to the air inside the balloon as it gets hotter.

10 Does the balloon push or pull on the beaker when the air inside the balloon gets hot?

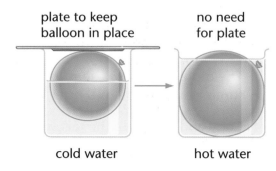

**WHAT YOU NEED TO REMEMBER** (Copy and complete using the **key words**)

**Other effects of heating and cooling**

If a solid or liquid or gas is heated, it will _____.

If we cool the solid or liquid or gas down, then it will _____.

Expanding materials produce _____ forces. Contracting materials produce _____ forces. These forces can be very large and cause lots of damage.

**More about warmer and colder: C1.5**

# 1.8 Looking at change

The diagrams show some of the ways substances can change.

1 Write down <u>five</u> different ways that substances can change.

Even though substances may change in some ways, other things about the substance may stay the same.

## ■ Does the mass of things change?

You can find the **mass** of something by weighing it.

The diagrams show the mass of some ice before and after melting.

2 (a) What was the mass of the ice cube before melting?

(b) What was the mass of the water after the ice had melted?

3 Copy and complete this sentence.

When ice changes to water, the _____ does not change.

> The number of grams of a substance is called its mass.

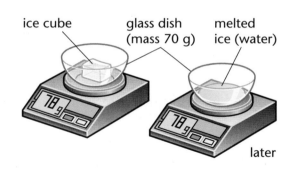

The diagrams show the mass of some salt and some water before and after they are mixed.

4 Copy and complete the following.

Before: mass of salt      = _____ g
        mass of water     = _____ g
After:  mass of salty water = _____ g

5 Copy and complete this sentence.

When one substance dissolves in another, the total _____ does not change.

The same thing happens with the other changes on this page.

When something changes there is still the same amount of stuff so the mass stays the same.

## Changing things back

Some changes are easy to change back. We say they are easy to **reverse**.

6 Write a sentence about the reverse of the changes in (a) and (b).

(a) You can change a solid to a liquid by heating it.

(b) You can change a gas to a liquid by cooling it.

7 Look at the diagrams.

(a) How can you get the <u>salt</u> back from salt solution?

(b) How can you get the <u>water</u> back from salt solution?

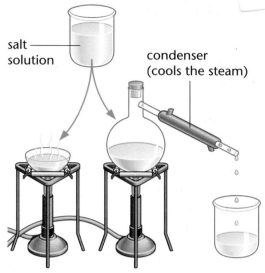

salt solution

condenser (cools the steam)

Boil off the water to get the salt.

To get the water, boil it off and condense it again; this is called distilling the water.

## Still the same stuff

When water freezes, boils, expands or dissolves salt, it is still water. No new substances are produced.

Changes which do not produce new substances are called **physical** changes.

Some physical changes are easy to reverse. Some are not easy to reverse.

8 Look at the pictures of breaking glass and melting ice.

(a) Why are these changes <u>physical</u> changes?

(b) Which physical change is easier to reverse?

breaking glass

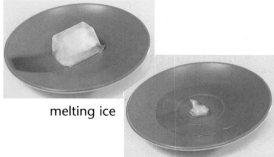

melting ice

**WHAT YOU NEED TO REMEMBER** (Copy and complete using the **key words**)

**Looking at change**

When things change, the _____ doesn't change.

Changes which don't produce new substances are called _____ changes.

Physical changes are usually easy to _____.

**More about changes: C2.1, C2.2**

# 2.1 Mixtures

Lots of things are **mixtures**.

**1** Write down the names of <u>two</u> mixtures.

*A mixture of different sweets.*

## Air is a mixture

The air you breathe is a mixture of **gases**.

Air also has some solids in it like dust, insects, birds and planes!

Air is mainly a mixture of the gases **oxygen** and **nitrogen**. Oxygen is the one we need to stay alive.

*A mixture of fruit and nuts.*

**2** Copy and complete this table.

| Gas in the air | Percentage |
|---|---|
| nitrogen | |
| | 21% |
| everything else | |

*Pie chart of gases in the air.*

Between these lines is 5%.  These dots mark every 1%.

everything else

oxygen

nitrogen

## Changing the mixture

You can change the **amount** of the things in a mixture. For example, in mixed fruit and nuts you can put more fruit and less nuts.

You change the mixture of gases in the air when you breathe. Your body picks the gas it needs out of the mixture of gases in the air.

**3** Which gas does your body take from the air when you breathe?

**4** Which gas do you add more of to the air when you breathe?

carbon dioxide

everything else

oxygen

nitrogen

*Pie chart of gases you breathe out.*

### What is in the sea

Sea-water is a mixture of lots of things. As well as fish and plants there is also salt.

A mixture of things can be **split** up. You can get the **salt** out of the sea by **evaporating** the water. The water goes into the air and leaves the salt behind.

5 (a) How do people get salt from the sea in hot countries?

(b) How much salt could you get from 1 kg of sea-water?

*Heat from the sun evaporates the water. Salt is left behind.*
*There are about 3.5 g of salt dissolved in each 100 g of sea-water.*

### How sea-water can be changed

You can change a mixture like sea-water by adding things to it.

Rivers carry substances to the sea. If a factory dumps poisonous waste into the river, the poison can damage sea life.

6 How can waste from an inland factory get into the sea?

7 Why is polluting the sea a bad idea?

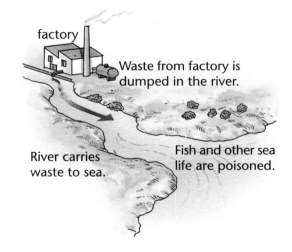

factory

Waste from factory is dumped in the river.

River carries waste to sea.

Fish and other sea life are poisoned.

**WHAT YOU NEED TO REMEMBER** (Copy and complete using the **key words**)

**Mixtures**

Air and sea-water are both _____.

Air is a mixture of _____. The two main gases in the air are _____ and _____.

The sea is a mixture of water, _____ and lots of other things. nitrogen

Mixtures can be _____ up into their different parts. For example, you can get the salt out of sea-water by _____ the water.

You can change the _____ of different things in a mixture.

**More about mixtures: C1.6**

## 2.2 Taking out the bits

We can use a **sieve** to separate peas from water.

1  Why does the sieve trap the peas?

2  What would happen if the sieve's holes were larger than the peas?

peas in water

sieve

peas

water

You need a sieve with very small holes to strain bits of fruit out when you make fruit jelly. Two pieces of cotton sheet make a good sieve.

3  Why is the cotton sheet better than an ordinary sieve?

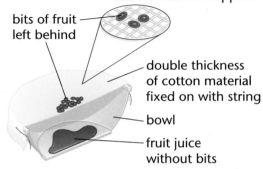

The juice goes through small holes in sheet, but the bits are trapped.

bits of fruit left behind

double thickness of cotton material fixed on with string

bowl

fruit juice without bits

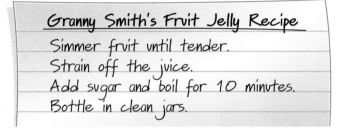

Granny Smith's Fruit Jelly Recipe

Simmer fruit until tender.
Strain off the juice.
Add sugar and boil for 10 minutes.
Bottle in clean jars.

### ■ Using paper

Kitchen paper has very tiny holes in it. They let liquids soak through. You can use kitchen paper to take bits of **solid** out of a liquid. You can also buy special paper to do this called filter paper.

Taking bits of solid out of a liquid like this is called **filtering**.

4  Copy the diagram. Then copy and complete this passage.

The liquid and bits of solid are poured into the _____ paper in the funnel.

The solid is trapped by the paper.
The solid is called the _____.

The liquid goes through the filter paper. It is called the filtrate.

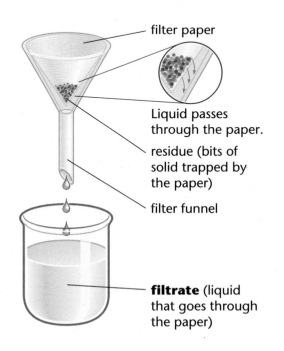

filter paper

Liquid passes through the paper.

residue (bits of solid trapped by the paper)

filter funnel

**filtrate** (liquid that goes through the paper)

## ■ Separating salt and pepper

You could use a magnifying glass and a pair of tweezers to **separate** salt and pepper. It would take a while!

Salt dissolves in water but pepper does not. This means you can separate them by filtering.

5 On a copy of the flow chart, write down these words in the correct boxes to show how to separate salt and pepper.

- Evaporate the water to get the salt.

- Filter.

- Stir salt and pepper in some water.

- Pepper stays on the filter paper.

## ■ What can you separate using filtration?

You can separate two things using filtering if one dissolves in a liquid but the other does not.

6 Which of these mixtures could you separate by stirring with water then filtering? (Use the information in the table. Give a reason for each answer.)

(a) salt and sand

(b) salt and sugar

(c) sugar and pepper

(d) pepper and sand

Put a teaspoon of salt and pepper in water and stir.

Strain through kitchen paper in a sieve.

Put the water on a sunny window sill for a few days.

salt left behind          pepper left on paper

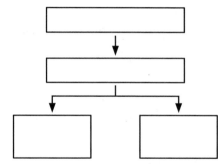

| Substance | Does it dissolve in water? |
|---|---|
| salt | dissolves in water |
| sand | does not dissolve in water |
| sugar | dissolves in water |
| pepper | does not dissolve in water |

**WHAT YOU NEED TO REMEMBER** (Copy and complete using the **key words**)

**Taking out the bits**

Filter paper acts like a very fine _____.

We can _____ a mixture of liquid and particles of solid using filter paper. We call this _____.

The _____ left behind in the filter paper is called the residue.

The liquid that goes through the filter paper is called the _____.

**More about separation: C1.7**

# 2.3 Getting the liquid back

A chef let his soup boil for too long. He was left with a pan of dried-up gunge and kitchen walls dripping with water.

1  What came out of the pan when the soup was boiling?

2  What stayed in the pan when the water boiled away?

3  Why did the water appear on the kitchen walls and windows?

earlier that day

The water has boiled to steam.

solid bits left behind

Cold windows and walls make steam change back to water (it condenses).

## ■ Getting drinking water from the sea

Sea water will poison you if you drink too much. This is because there is so much salt and other solid substances dissolved in it.

When we boil sea water, the water **boils** and turns into steam but the **solids** do not boil. We can **condense** the steam back into water. 'Condense' means change from gas to liquid.

4  What comes out of sea water as it boils?

5  What happens when the steam meets the cold wall of the beaker?

6  What substance collects on the wall of the beaker?

7  What would be left in the dish if you heated it until it dried up?

We can get drinking water from sea water by boiling it. We can condense the steam and collect the water. This water is pure and you can drink it. It is called **distilled** water. To make enough distilled water to drink we need something better than a beaker.

8  Can you use a beaker to condense steam for a long time? Explain your answer.

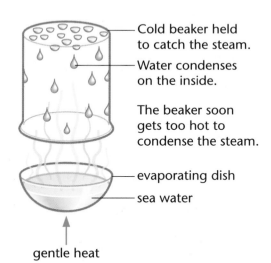

Cold beaker held to catch the steam.

Water condenses on the inside.

The beaker soon gets too hot to condense the steam.

evaporating dish

sea water

gentle heat

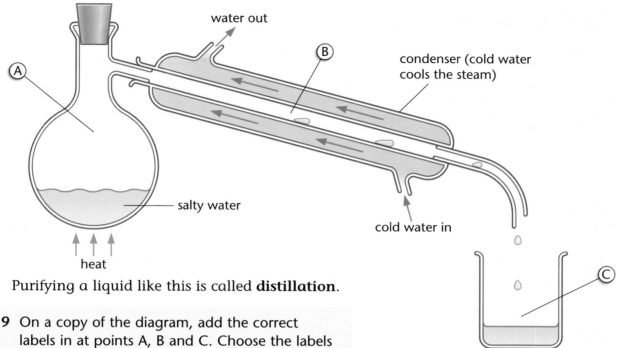

water out

(A)

(B)

condenser (cold water cools the steam)

salty water

cold water in

heat

(C)

Purifying a liquid like this is called **distillation**.

*Distilling sea water.*

**9** On a copy of the diagram, add the correct labels in at points A, B and C. Choose the labels from this list.

- Pure water is collected.

- The water changes to steam and the salt is left behind.

- The steam condenses to water.

evaporation

↓ = distillation

condensation

## When do you use distillation?

You use distillation to get a pure liquid when things are dissolved in it.
You use filtering to separate a solid from a liquid when they are not dissolved.

**10** Copy the table, then complete it.

| Mixture | What is wanted | Method of separation |
|---|---|---|
| sand and water | sand | |
| sugar dissolved in water | water | |

**WHAT YOU NEED TO REMEMBER** (Copy and complete using the **key words**)

**Getting the liquid back**

When a solid dissolves in water we can get the water back by _____.

This works because the water _____ and turns into steam.

The steam is cooled to _____ it.

The _____ get left behind.

The water we get at the end is pure. It is called _____ water.

**More about separating mixtures: C1.8**

# 2.4 What's in a colour?

A pure dye contains only one colour. Black ink is made from two or more coloured dyes mixed together.

The pictures show one way of separating the dyes.

1 How does the water reach the ink spot?

2 What happens to the ink spot as the water soaks across the paper?

3 What different dyes are used to make black ink?

## ■ A better way of separating the dyes

Separating substances like this is called <u>chromatography</u>. The pattern of colours you get is called a **chromatogram**.

4 Which inks are made from only one dye?

5 What colours are in the green ink?

## ■ Who forged the cheque?

A chromatogram was made from the ink on a forged cheque.

Chromatograms were made from the pens used by two suspects.

6 (a) Who do you think forged the cheque?

(b) Does the chromatogram prove beyond doubt who forged the cheque?

(Give reasons for your answers.)

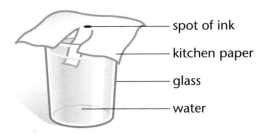

*Using water to separate ink colours.*

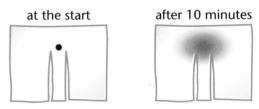

*After 10 minutes the paper can be dried and the colours seen.*

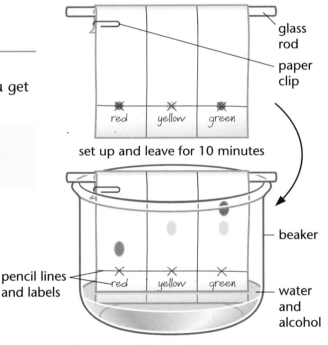

*Colours in different inks.*

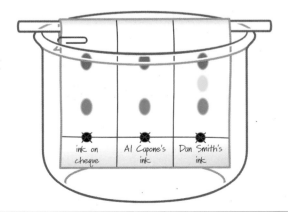

## Spreading at different speeds

Chromatography is used to split up a mixture of substances that **dissolve** in the same liquid. The substances spread across the paper at different **speeds**.

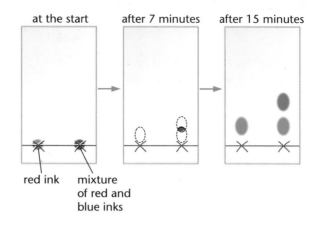

at the start    after 7 minutes    after 15 minutes

red ink    mixture of red and blue inks

7 Copy the diagram. Use coloured pens to copy the spots shown at the start and after 15 minutes. Then colour in the spots for after 7 minutes.

## More inks

Chromatography was used to split up some inks. A mixture of alcohol and water was used because all the inks would dissolve in it.

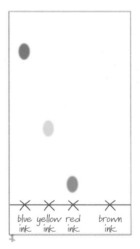

blue ink    yellow ink    red ink    brown ink

8 Brown ink is made from a mixture of yellow, blue and red inks. Copy the diagram and complete the section for the brown ink.

9 Why was a mixture of alcohol and water used to make the chromatogram?

10 Which inks shown on the diagram are made from only one colour?

### WHAT YOU NEED TO REMEMBER (Copy and complete using the key words)

**What's in a colour?**

Chromatography is used to split up a mixture of substances that _____ in the same liquid.

The substances spread out through the paper at different _____.

The pattern you get is called a _____.

**More about separating mixtures: C1.8**

# 2.5 Elements

There are about 750 000 words in the English language and they are all made out of just 26 letters joined together in different ways.

**1** How many English words can you make from the letters E, I, L, and V? You don't have to use all the letters, and letters can be repeated.

**Elements** are substances that cannot be split into anything **simpler**. There are about 90 elements on the Earth.

All the other substances in the world are made from these elements joined together just like all the words are made from 26 letters.

**2** What is the name for a substance that cannot be split into simpler substances?

**3** About how many elements make up the substances on the Earth?

## ■ Is water an element?

Until the year 1800, people thought water was an element but they were wrong.

The diagram shows how we know that they were wrong.

**4** What two elements make up water?

**5** How can water be split up into its elements?

**6** How can you tell that an electric current flows in the circuit?

**7** Why was it impossible to do this experiment before 1794?

About 90 elements make millions of substances.

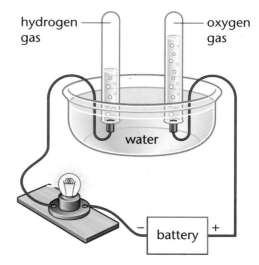

In 1800 an electric current was passed through water for the first time. The current splits the water into its elements.

### DID YOU KNOW?

An electric current was first discovered in 1794.

## Elements on the Earth

Some elements are more common than others.

**8** Which <u>three</u> elements are the most common ones in the Earth's crust?

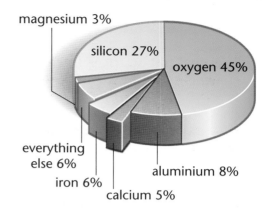

*Pie chart showing elements in the Earth's crust.*

magnesium 3%
silicon 27%
oxygen 45%
everything else 6%
iron 6%
calcium 5%
aluminium 8%

## Elements in common substances

Look at the chart of substances.

Carbon is an element. It is made of only one thing, carbon.

Water is not an element. It is made of two elements joined together, **hydrogen** and **oxygen**.

| Substance | What is in it |
|---|---|
| water | hydrogen, oxygen |
| carbon | carbon |
| salt | sodium, chlorine |
| oxygen | oxygen |
| carbon dioxide | carbon, oxygen |
| limestone | calcium, carbon, oxygen |
| iron | iron |
| gold | gold |

| Substance | What is in it |
|---|---|
| sugar | carbon, hydrogen, oxygen |
| natural gas | carbon, hydrogen |
| sulphur | sulphur |
| magnesium oxide | magnesium, oxygen |
| nitrogen | nitrogen |
| copper | copper |
| iron sulphide | iron, sulphur |
| butane | carbon, hydrogen |

**9** Copy out the heading of the table below. Complete it using the information above.

| Some substances that are elements |
|---|
|  |

### DID YOU KNOW?

When elements are joined together, we say they are <u>combined</u>.

## WHAT YOU NEED TO REMEMBER (Copy and complete using the **key words**)

**Elements**

An element is a substance that cannot be split into anything _____.

Water is made from the two elements _____ and _____.

Altogether there are about 90 _____ that make up everything else.

**More about elements: C2.3**

# 2.6 Shorthand for elements

Scientists put all the elements into a special chart. On the chart each element has a **symbol**.

**1** Copy the table. Then write the names of the elements by the symbols shown in the table.

| Name of element | Symbol |
|---|---|
| | C |
| | S |
| | H |
| | O |
| | P |
| | Al |

**2** What do you notice about the symbol for each of these elements and its name?

Each symbol begins with a **capital** letter.

Sometimes we need to use a second letter. For example, N is the symbol for nitrogen. So we use the symbol Ne for neon. The second letter is always a small letter.

**3** Copy and complete the table.

| Name of element | Symbol |
|---|---|
| helium | |
| magnesium | |
| zinc | |
| chlorine | |
| copper | |

The symbols for some elements are nothing like their names.

**4** **(a)** What is the symbol for iron?

**(b)** Why does it have this symbol?

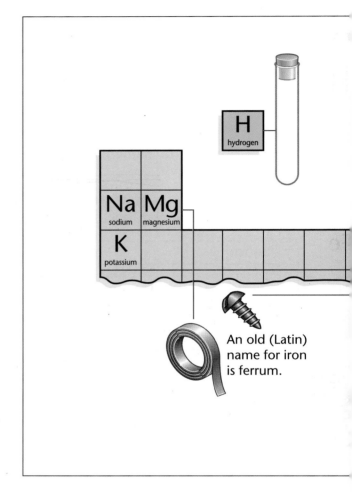

An old (Latin) name for iron is ferrum.

**5** Copy and complete the table using the chart of elements to help you.

| Name of element | Symbol |
|---|---|
| potassium | |
| | Au |
| sodium | |

art of a scientist's chart of the elements

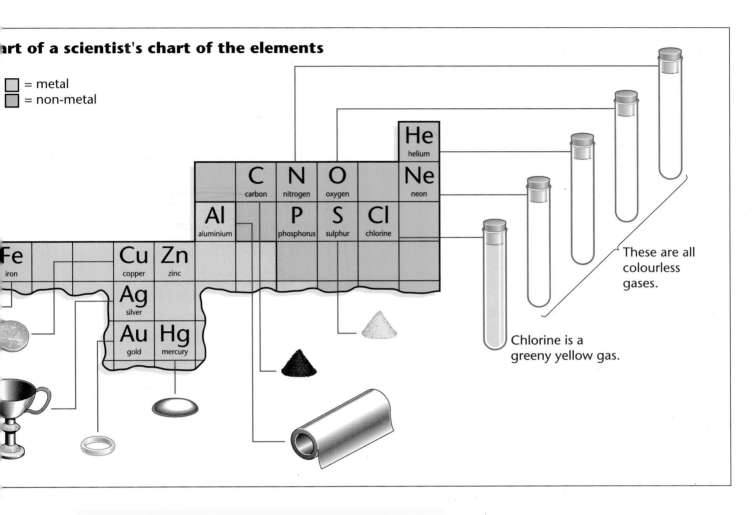

☐ = metal
☐ = non-metal

These are all colourless gases.

Chlorine is a greeny yellow gas.

6  Which element is a yellow solid but not a metal?

7  Write down the name of a gas which is coloured.

8  (a)  Write down one thing that is the same about all the metals in the picture.

   (b)  Write down one thing that is different about some metals.

**WHAT YOU NEED TO REMEMBER** (Copy and complete using the **key words**)

**Shorthand for elements**

Every element has a _____. This is either one or two letters.

The first letter is always a _____ letter.

More about elements: C2.3

# 2.7 Putting elements together

Everything on the Earth is made from the elements. Sometimes the elements are found by themselves in the ground or in the air.

Use a copy of the scientists' chart of elements to help you answer these questions. Look back at pages 36–37 if you can't remember what the symbols stand for.

**1** Which substances in the picture are elements?

This prospector is looking for gold.

A substance made from different elements joined together (combined) is called a **compound**.

**2** Which substances in the picture are compounds?

Compounds have very different **properties** from the elements they are made from.

**3** Copy and complete the table using the information in the box and the pictures.

| Name of compound | Elements in the compound |
|---|---|
| water | |
| salt (sodium chloride) | |

**4** Describe one way in which water is different from both the elements it contains.

**5** Describe one way in which salt is different from the two elements it contains.

**REMEMBER** from pages 36–37

Scientists use a special chart of the elements.

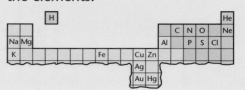

Air contains oxygen, nitrogen and carbon dioxide gases.

Clouds are made from tiny water droplets.

Ayers Rock in Australia is sandstone containing iron oxide (iron joined with oxygen).

There are tiny specks of gold mixed with the rock and dust.

## DID YOU KNOW?

Water is hydrogen combined with oxygen. Water is a liquid and does not burn. Hydrogen and oxygen are gases. They make a mixture that can burn or even explode.

These are dangerous substances.

sodium metal + chlorine gas

crystals of sodium chloride

## Making compounds

Iron and sulphur are both elements.

6  Describe what the fresh iron filings look like.

7  Describe what the sulphur looks like.

8  What must you do to make the iron and the sulphur join together to make a compound?

9  Write down <u>two</u> ways in which the new compound is different from what we started with.

*If iron and sulphur are mixed together and heated, a new substance is made.*

## Compounds from burning

When iron and sulphur join together we say that a **chemical** reaction has happened. Burning is also a type of chemical reaction. When an element burns a compound is formed.

10  What does the magnesium look like:

(a)  before burning,

(b)  after burning?

11  Which other element takes part in the reaction when magnesium burns?

12  What is the name of the new compound formed when magnesium burns?

Although there are only about 90 elements, there are lots of different ways of putting them together. This means that there are millions of different compounds.

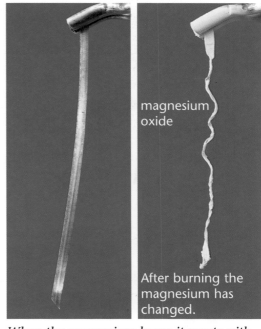

*When the magnesium burns it reacts with oxygen from the air.*

---

**WHAT YOU NEED TO REMEMBER**  (Copy and complete using the **key words**)

**Putting elements together**

A substance which contains two or more elements joined together (combined) is called a _____.

Compounds have different _____ from the elements they contain.

Many compounds are formed by _____ reactions between elements.

**More about compounds: C2.4**

# 2.8 Useful compounds

**Water** is probably the liquid that we know best. It is also the most useful compound known.

1 Make a list of the things that we use water for. The illustration gives some ideas.

*Using water.*

## ■ Using salt

**Salt** is also a very useful compound. Salt is a solid. It has been prized by people for a long time.

2 Look at the pictures. Write down a list of things that people use salt for.

Today we can make lots of other **compounds** from salt.

3 Look at the pictures. Write down <u>two</u> other compounds that we make from salt.

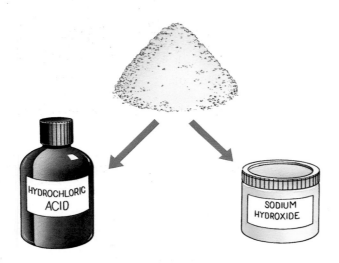

*Using salt as a preservative.*

*Using salt as a flavouring.*

*Using salt to help thaw ice on roads.*

## A compound in the air

Carbon dioxide is a gas. Small amounts are present in the air. Carbon dioxide is a very important compound.

**4** Write down <u>two</u> uses of carbon dioxide.

*Two uses of carbon dioxide.*

 Find out the properties of carbon dioxide which allow it to be used in these ways.

Whenever **carbon** burns in air, it usually makes carbon dioxide.

The charcoal fuel that we burn in barbecues is mainly carbon.

**5** Copy and complete the word equation below that shows what happens when carbon burns.

carbon + oxygen → _____ di_____

Most fuels have carbon in them.

**6** Write down the names of <u>five</u> other fuels which contain carbon.

When these fuels burn, they make the same gas.

**7** Write down the name of this gas.

natural gas

petrol

wood

carbon dioxide

heating oil

charcoal

coal

*Examples of fuels which contain carbon.*

## WHAT YOU NEED TO REMEMBER (Copy and complete using the **key words**)

**Useful compounds**

The best-known liquid in the world is _____.

A solid compound used to make lots of other substances is _____.

Air contains small amounts of _____ dioxide gas.

Water, salt and carbon dioxide are all very important _____.

**More about compounds: C2.4**

# 3.1 Looking at metals

We use metals for many different things. The pictures show what we use some metals for.

**1** Write down the names of <u>five</u> metals.

### ■ What do we know about metals?

There are many different metals. But most metals are like each other in lots of ways.

**2** Choose one word or phrase from each pair that describes what <u>most</u> metals are like.

    **(a)** soft / hard

    **(b)** weak / strong

    **(c)** shiny / dull

    **(d)** tough / brittle

    **(e)** heavy or dense / light

    **(f)** conduct heat / do not conduct heat

    **(g)** conduct electricity / do not conduct electricity

    **(h)** liquid / solid

> We usually talk about 'heat', but the correct technical term is 'thermal energy'.

The words you have chosen (like 'hard' and 'strong') describe the <u>properties</u> of metals.

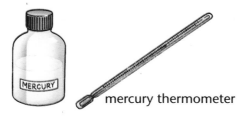

mercury thermometer

*Mercury is the only metal that is not a solid at ordinary temperatures.*

*Steel is **hard** and strong.*

*Aluminium is shiny.*

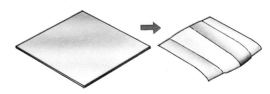

    steel sheet           car bonnet

*Steel is tough and can be stamped into different shapes without breaking.*

brass                    iron

*Metal weights.*

aluminium

heat travels through the metal from the flames

*Metals **conduct** heat.*

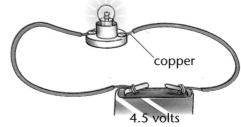

copper

4.5 volts

*Metals conduct **electricity**.*

## Sorting out metals

People who work in scrap-yards sort out metals from other materials.

3 Copy the table. Then match each material with one of the parts of the scrap car.

| Material | Part of car |
|----------|-------------|
| plastic  |             |
| steel    |             |
| glass    |             |
| rubber   |             |

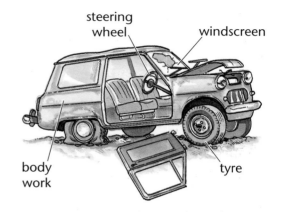

steering wheel  windscreen
body work  tyre

## Working with scrap metals

People who work in scrap-yards must also sort out different metals from each other.

We use more steel than any other metal. Steel is made mainly of iron. Both iron and steel are **magnetic**. We can pick them up with a magnet. Most other metals are not magnetic.

4 Which objects in the drawing would a magnetic crane <u>not</u> pick up?

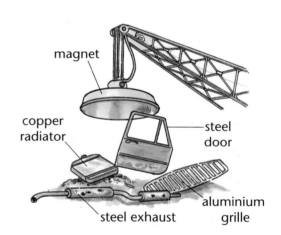

magnet
copper radiator
steel door
steel exhaust
aluminium grille

## Metals and non-metals

There are millions of different substances in the world around us. They are made up of about 90 very simple substances that we call elements, joined together in different ways.

Most of these elements are metals. The rest of the elements are <u>non-metals</u>.

**WHAT YOU NEED TO REMEMBER** (Copy and complete using the **key words**)

**Looking at metals**

Metals are normally shiny and _____.

Metals conduct _____.

Metals _____ heat.

Iron and steel are _____.

**More about metals: C1.2**

# 3.2 Non-metals

Most of the elements are metals. But about a quarter of all the elements in nature are not metals. We call them **non-metals**.

Non-metals are a very mixed bunch!

The pictures show some of the non-metals at 20°C.

As you can see, non-metals are very different from each other. For example, some are solids, one is a liquid and some are **gases.**

**REMEMBER** from page 34

Everything is made from some different elements joined together in different ways. There are about 90 elements found on Earth.

Sulphur.

Iodine.

Bromine

Chlorine

Hydrogen

Nitrogen

Oxygen

Phosphorus

You must keep this under water.

**1** Copy the headings:

Solid          Liquid          Gas

**(a)** Now write down the names of the non-metallic elements under the correct headings.

**(b)** Write down the colour of each element under the name, for example:      hydrogen (colourless)

Carbon. (diamond)

Carbon. (graphite)

## USEFUL RULE

Any element that is a **gas** at room temperature is also a non-metal.

### ■ How do we know if an element is a metal or a non-metal?

The biggest difference between metals and non-metals is that most non-metals do <u>not</u> **conduct** heat or electricity.

2  Look at the diagram. Copy and complete the sentence.

Sulphur does not conduct _____.

Carbon, in the form of graphite, does conduct electricity. This is very unusual for a non-metal.

3  Copy and complete the sentence.

Carbon does not conduct _____.

The proper name for heat is thermal energy.
Non-metals are poor conductors of thermal energy.

### ■ Another difference between metals and non-metals

Most metals can be bent many times before they break. Lead is a metal.

4  What happens when you hit (a) the lead strip and (b) the carbon rod?

Most non-metal solids break easily when you hit them. We say they are **brittle**.

**REMEMBER** from page 42

Metals let heat and electricity pass through them easily. We say they conduct heat and electricity.

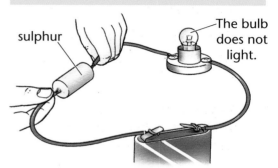

sulphur

The bulb does not light.

*Does sulphur conduct electricity?*

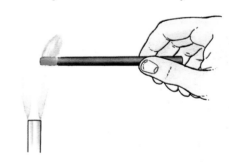

*The carbon burns but the other end of the carbon rod does not get hot.*

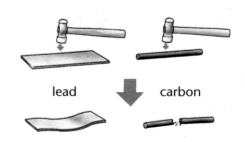

lead                    carbon

### WHAT YOU NEED TO REMEMBER (Copy and complete using the **key words**)

**Non-metals**

Elements that are not metals are called _____.

Non-metals can be solids, liquids, or _____.

If we know an element is a _____, then we also know that it is a non-metal.

Most non-metals do not _____ heat or electricity.

Solid non-metals are _____.

**More about non-metals: C1.2**

# 3.3  Where do we find non-metals?

There aren't as many non-metals as metals. But most of the things around us are made from **non-metals**.

The pie chart shows that your body contains 3% of metals. The rest of you is made up of non-metals.

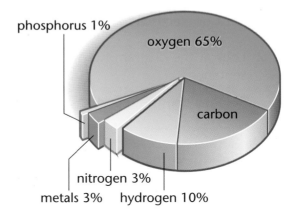

*The elements in your body.*
*(The percentages add up to 100.)*

1 What is the percentage of non-metals in the human body: 30% or 97% or 27% or 3%?

2 **(a)** What is the most common element in your body?

**(b)** What percentage of your body is made of this element?

The most important element in living things is **carbon**. All life is based on the element carbon.

3 **(a)** What percentage of your body is made up of carbon?

**(b)** How many times more carbon is there in your body than nitrogen?

## DID YOU KNOW?

Phosphorus is so reactive that we store it under water. When phosphorus comes into contact with air, it bursts into flames.

■ **Non-metals in food and drink**

The things we eat and drink are made mostly of non-metals.

4 Write down the names of <u>three</u> non-metals that are found both in Coca Cola and in your body.

5 Why does it seem strange to find phosphorus in our bodies?

Coca Cola is mainly water but also contains phosphoric acid; this is made of hydrogen, phosphorus and oxygen.

Your body needs phosphorus to make its cells work.

Most of your body is made up of water; this contains hydrogen and oxygen.

## ■ Non-metals in the air

The air around us is made from non-metals.

Look at the pie chart.

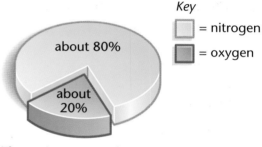

Key

□ = nitrogen

■ = oxygen

**6** What are the two main gases we find in air?

**7** What is the percentage of oxygen in the air?

*The main gases in the air.*

Now look at the drawings.

Without oxygen, **burning** could not take place.

Without **oxygen**, we could not breathe.

If more than 25% of the air were oxygen, then fire would have destroyed all the trees.

**8** Which element do we use when we breathe in?

**9** Which element is needed for things to burn?

**10** Nitrogen makes the air safe for living things. How does nitrogen do this?

## ■ Non-metals in the sea

The table shows the four most common elements in sea-water.

**11** Copy and complete:

The three most common elements in sea-water are all _____.

| Elements in sea-water | Approximate % |
|---|---|
| oxygen | 86 |
| hydrogen | 11 |
| chlorine | 2 |
| sodium | 1 |

*(Look back to page 44 if you can't remember whether these elements are solids, liquids or gases at ordinary temperatures.)*

---

**WHAT YOU NEED TO REMEMBER** (Copy and complete using the **key words**)

**Where do we find non-metals?**

Most of the things around us are made from _____.

Life is based on a non-metal called _____.

We need to breathe a non-metal called _____.

Oxygen is also needed for _____.

**More about non-metals: C1.2**

47

# 3.4 Elements of Thar

A star-ship left Earth to look for planets of distant stars. It found a planet called Thar.

Tharian scientists only know 15 of the elements. They don't even know about metals or non-metals.

**REMEMBER** from pages 42 and 44

Metals conduct **heat** and **electricity**.

Any element that is a **gas** must be a **non-metal**.

## ■ Metal or non-metal?

Earth scientists tell the Tharians about the different properties of metals and non-metals.

**1** Copy the table. Then complete it to show what the Earth scientists tell the Tharians.

| Test | Metal | Non-metal |
|---|---|---|
| Does it conduct heat? | | no |
| Does it conduct electricity? | yes | |

**2** Some elements are gases. What kind of element must a gas be – metal or non-metal?

**3** The drawing shows six of the Tharian elements being tested. Copy out the table. Then complete it to show the results of the tests.

| Thar element | Metal or non-metal? |
|---|---|
| cinz | |
| himule | |
| hongdery | |
| pulshur | |
| rolechin | |
| roni | |

## Elements and symbols on Thar

Earth scientists write out the list of 15 Tharian elements using Earth names.

They make one table for the gases and another table for the solid elements.

For the solid elements, they write down whether the element is a conductor or not.

The Earth scientists show the Tharians that these 15 elements are part of their own chart of the elements.

4  Copy the Earth scientists' chart of elements shown below. Write the symbols of the metals in blue and non-metals in red.

5  A Tharian element has the same letters in its name as the English name, but they are mixed up. Write down English names for:

cinz, himule, hongdery, pulshur, rolechin, roni.

| Gases | Symbol |
|---|---|
| hydrogen | H |
| helium | He |
| nitrogen | N |
| oxygen | O |
| chlorine | Cl |

| Solid element | Symbol | Conductor? |
|---|---|---|
| carbon | C | no |
| sodium | Na | yes |
| magnesium | Mg | yes |
| aluminium | Al | yes |
| phosphorus | P | no |
| sulphur | S | no |
| calcium | Ca | yes |
| iron | Fe | yes |
| copper | Cu | yes |
| zinc | Zn | yes |

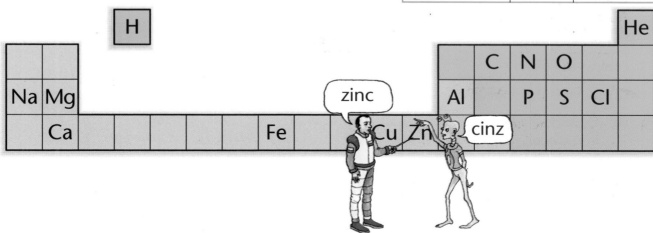

**WHAT YOU NEED TO REMEMBER** (Copy and complete using the **key words**)

**Elements of Thar**

An element is a metal or a _____.

Any element that is a _____ must be a non-metal.

We can test if an element is a metal or a non-metal. Metals conduct _____ and _____. Most non-metals do not conduct.

**More about metals and non-metals: C1.2**

# 3.5 Metals reacting with oxygen

When we set off a sparkler, the sparks are tiny bits of burning iron. These are so hot that they burn as they fly through the air. Iron and oxygen (from the air) join together to make a new substance we call <u>iron oxide</u>. This is a chemical reaction.

*iron + oxygen → iron oxide*

1 **(a)** What do you see when iron and oxygen react together?

**(b)** What new substance is produced?

### ■ Shooting stars, nature's sparklers

*Some shooting stars fall to the ground as meteorites.*

If you look at the sky when it's dark, you might see shooting stars. These are lumps of material from space. They mostly burn up as they go through the air.

But bigger lumps don't burn up completely so they hit the ground. We call them <u>meteorites</u>.

2 Are you more likely to see a shooting star during the daytime or during the night-time?

3 Look at the picture.

**(a)** What is the meteorite mainly made of?

**(b)** Explain why the meteorite has an outer layer of iron oxide.

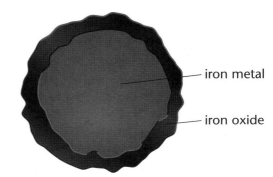

iron metal

iron oxide

*A meteorite cut in half (a cross-section).*

### ■ The beginning of the Iron Age

The first iron that people ever used came from meteorites. By heating the meteorite until it was red hot, Early Iron Age people could shape the iron into tools and weapons.

When red-hot iron is hammered, it gives off lots of sparks. These sparks are iron burning in **oxygen** from the air.

4 What is the same about the chemical reactions in the sparkler, the shooting star and the blacksmith pictures?

*A blacksmith hammering red-hot iron.*

## Artificial shooting stars

If a ship at sea is in trouble at night, a flare can be used to show rescuers where the ship is. The flare contains a metal called magnesium. Magnesium burns with a very bright flame:

magnesium + oxygen → magnesium oxide

5 What are the flares for?

6 Why is magnesium used in the flares rather than iron?

7 What chemical reaction occurs when magnesium burns?

*A rescue flare burns with a bright white light.*

## Reactions of metals with oxygen

A teacher heats iron, magnesium and copper. The teacher then puts the metals into gas jars filled with oxygen. The diagram shows the reactions.

8 (a) Which metal burns brightest?

(b) Which metal burns dullest?

We say that metals that burn brightest are the most **reactive**.

9 Which is the most reactive of these three metals?

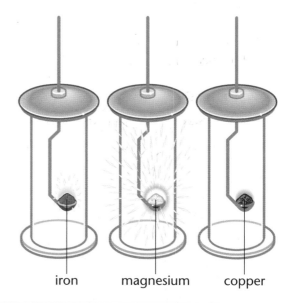

iron　　magnesium　　copper

**WHAT YOU NEED TO REMEMBER** (Copy and complete using the **key words**)

**Metals reacting with oxygen**

A few metals burn very easily in the air's _____.

Metals that burn brightest are the most _____.

**More about reacting with oxygen: C2.5**

# 3.6 Metals reacting with water

## ■ Does copper react with water?

In days gone by, people used **copper** kettles to boil water. Nowadays, we use copper pipes to carry hot water to the radiators that keep rooms warm.

1 Do you think that copper reacts with water or steam? Give a reason for your answer.

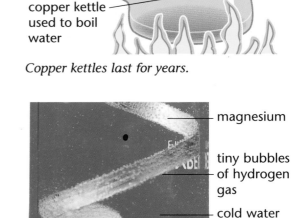

*Copper kettles last for years.*

## ■ Magnesium reacting with water

Remember how magnesium burns in air? That was a very fast reaction. Magnesium also reacts with cold **water** but only very slowly.

2 (a) How can you see that a reaction is taking place?

   (b) What gas is made in the reaction?

*Magnesium reacts very slowly with cold water.*

The reaction goes very quickly if we put burning magnesium into **steam**.

3 Why do you think the reaction is faster in steam than in cold water?

4 Which metal, copper or magnesium, is more reactive?

5 What <u>two</u> new substances are made in the reaction between magnesium and steam?

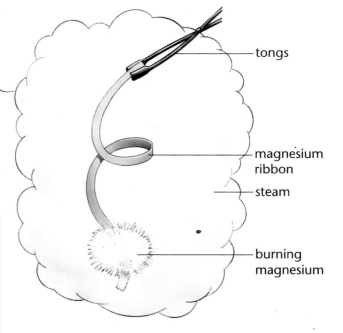

*Magnesium burns in steam. Hydrogen and magnesium oxide are the two new substances made in this chemical reaction.*

## Sodium – a strange metal

**Sodium** is an unusual metal. Sodium is so soft that you can cut it with an ordinary table knife. It is so light that it floats on water.

Sodium is very reactive. It reacts very quickly with cold water. The reaction makes **hydrogen** gas.

Sodium will even react with the water vapour in the air. So we store sodium in oil.

*sodium + water → sodium hydroxide + hydrogen*

6 You must never pick sodium up with bare hands. Why do you think this is so?

7 Why is sodium stored in oil?

8 Which metal is more reactive, copper or sodium? Explain your answer.

9 Which metal is more reactive, magnesium or sodium? Explain your answer.

oil

SODIUM

## Metals for kettles

10 We can make a kettle out of copper. Could we make a kettle out of sodium or magnesium? Explain your answers.

11 Write out the three metals below, in order of their reactivity. Put the most reactive first, and the least reactive last.

    copper       magnesium       sodium

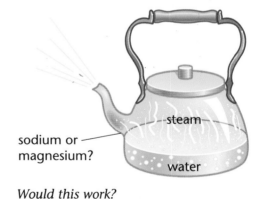

steam

sodium or magnesium?

water

*Would this work?*

## WHAT YOU NEED TO REMEMBER (Copy and complete using the **key words**)

**Metals reacting with water**

Some metals, for example magnesium:
- react slowly with _____;
- react more quickly with _____.

A few metals react quickly with water, for example _____.

All these reactions make a gas called _____.

Some metals do not react with water, for example _____.

**More about reactivity: CORE+ C2.17**

53

# 3.7 Which metals push hardest?

The main aim of the gladiators is to **push** the other gladiator off the platform.

A big gladiator can usually push much harder than a small gladiator.

1 If one gladiator is much bigger than the other, what result do you expect?

Metals behave like the gladiators. A reactive metal will try to 'push around' a less reactive metal.

In any fight between the two metals, we expect the more reactive metal to win.

2 Look at the copper and iron 'gladiators'. Which one will win?

*Iron Maiden clobbers Copper Princess.*

### ■ Can you coat a knife with copper?

Jill puts an old penknife blade into copper sulphate solution for two minutes. She then takes it out and looks at it.

3 (a) What did the blade look like before?

(b) What does the blade look like after?

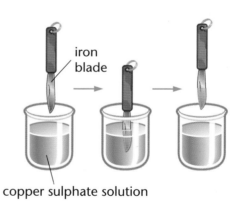

copper sulphate solution

Iron is more reactive than copper. So iron pushes copper out of copper sulphate.

We say that the iron **displaces** the copper. It takes the place of the copper in the copper sulphate.

*iron + copper sulphate → iron sulphate + copper*

### ■ Where does the copper go?

The reaction makes a very thin layer of copper on the knife blade. If you scratch it, you can see the iron still underneath.

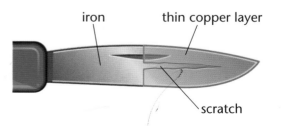

### ■ Can you coat a penny with iron?

Jill puts a bright, shiny, copper coin into iron sulphate solution for two minutes. She then takes it out and looks at it.

**4** Has the coin changed?

Copper cannot push iron out of the iron sulphate because copper is less reactive than iron. So the coin does not change. There isn't a **displacement** reaction.

**5** How does the copper behave in this reaction – like a small gladiator or big gladiator?

### ■ A three metal contest

Jill puts a strip of magnesium ribbon into a test-tube of iron sulphate and another strip into copper sulphate solution. After two minutes she takes the strips out.

**6** What changes can you see? Copy and complete the table.

| Name of solution | What the magnesium looks like | |
|---|---|---|
| | before the reaction | after the reaction |
| copper sulphate | silvery | |
| iron sulphate | | black layer |

**7** Copy and complete the sentences.

Magnesium displaces copper from _____ sulphate solution and iron from _____ sulphate solution. So magnesium is more _____ than both copper and iron.

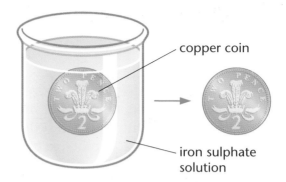

copper coin

iron sulphate solution

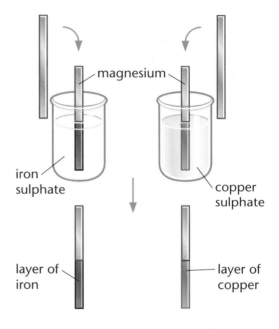

magnesium

iron sulphate

copper sulphate

layer of iron

layer of copper

---

### WHAT YOU NEED TO REMEMBER (Copy and complete using the **key words**)

**Which metals push hardest?**

A reactive metal has a bigger _____ than a less reactive metal.
A reactive metal _____ a less reactive metal. We call this a _____ reaction.

**More about displacement: C2.7**

# 3.8 Which metals react best?

Chemists look at the reactions of metals with oxygen and water. They also look at the displacement reactions of the metals. They then put the metals into a list in order of their **reactivity**. The <u>most</u> reactive go near the **top** and the <u>least</u> reactive go near the **bottom**. We call this list the **reactivity series**.

| sodium |
| magnesium |     reactivity decreases |
| iron |
| copper |

*The reactivity series for the metals we have looked at so far.*

## ■ Using the reactivity series

If we know where a metal is in the reactivity series, we can work out how it will react. We can do this before we even see the reactions. We call this **predicting**.

Chlorine is a very reactive gas. Most metals react with chlorine. But some will react better than others.

**Chlorine is a <u>very</u> dangerous gas.**

Only your teacher should use it. The following experiments also need to be done in a fume cupboard.

1 Which of the metals sodium, iron or copper do you expect to burn brightest in chlorine? Which do you expect to burn dullest?

2 The pictures show what actually happens. Write down the names of the three metals in order. Start with the metal that burns brightest in chlorine and finish with the one that burns least well.

3 Did your prediction agree with what really happens?

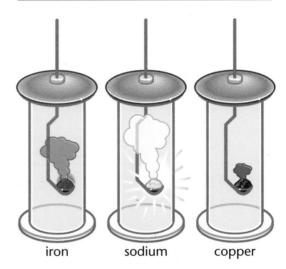

iron            sodium            copper

*Metals burning in chlorine.*

## ■ Adding more elements to the series

As you learn about more metals you can add them to the reactivity series.

4 (a) Potassium is more reactive than sodium. Copy the reactivity series from the top of the page. Then add potassium to it.

(b) Silver is a less reactive metal than copper. Add silver to your reactivity series.

### Making electricity out of a lemon

You can make electricity if you put two different metals into acid.

The diagram shows how Billy did this.

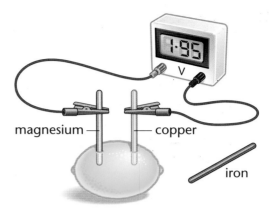

You can make electricity like this because a lemon contains acid.

5  How do you know Billy made electricity?

6  As well as the magnesium and copper rods, Billy can use iron. Draw two other batteries that Billy can make using the lemon.

7  Billy's teacher did not let him use sodium. Why not?

**REMEMBER** from page 53

Sodium is a very reactive metal. It reacts so fast with water that it's dangerous.

### Which battery is best?

You get a bigger voltage if the two different metals are a long way apart in the reactivity series.

Billy made three different batteries using copper, magnesium and iron. He labelled them A, B and C.

He measured the volts for each battery. He got:

0.5 volts,   1.5 volts,   2.0 volts.

8  Match up these voltages with the batteries A, B and C.

9  Which pair of metals did Billy use for battery A? (Hint. Look at the diagram at the top of this page.)

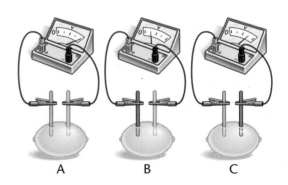

A          B          C

---

**WHAT YOU NEED TO REMEMBER**  (Copy and complete using the **key words**)

**Which metals react best?**

We can list metals in order of _____. This list is called the _____ _____.

We put the most reactive at the _____ of the list, and the least reactive at the _____.

The reactivity series is useful for _____ how a metal will react.

**More about metal reactions: C2.5, C2.6, C2.7**

# 4.1 Chemical changes

When you see something change, ask yourself:

'Has the change really made anything new?'

If the change makes a **new** substance, then it is a <u>chemical</u> change. If the change does <u>not</u> make a new substance, then it is a <u>physical</u> change.

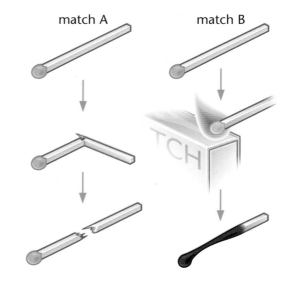

## ■ Playing with fire

Jane has two matches, A and B. She breaks match A into two. She strikes match B and it lights. After burning, match B is black.

1 (a) Which change makes new substances?

(b) Which is a chemical change?

## ■ Dissolving

When we put sugar into a glass of water and stir, the sugar seems to disappear. We say the sugar <u>dissolves</u>. We know the sugar is there because the water tastes sweet.

If we leave this for a few days, the water dries up – it <u>evaporates</u>. We can see crystals of sugar in the bottom of the glass.

Dissolving sugar in water is a physical change.

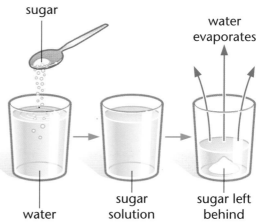

2 Why is dissolving sugar in water not a chemical change?

## ■ Do metals dissolve in acids?

If we add magnesium to dilute hydrochloric acid the magnesium does more than dissolve. It reacts with the acid to make new substances.

3 (a) What two new substances does this reaction make?

(b) Is it a physical or chemical change?

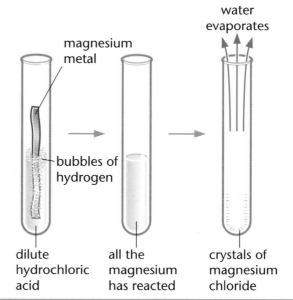

## Chemical changes in living things

Chemical changes don't just happen in test-tubes. Every living thing needs **chemical** changes to stay alive.

For an egg to hatch into a baby chicken there must be lots of chemical changes.

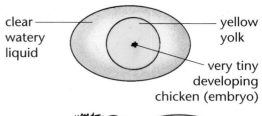

clear watery liquid

yellow yolk

very tiny developing chicken (embryo)

The chicken has feathers, bones, skin, blood, ...

**4** When a chicken grows inside the egg,

  **(a)** what are the starting materials?

  **(b)** what new substances are made?

**5** Why is the growth of a chicken inside an egg called a chemical change?

## Chemical changes in us

We eat all sorts of food to stay healthy. But before our bodies can use food, it must be broken down into simpler substances. This is called <u>digestion</u>.

To stay alive, our bodies must make chemical changes all the time.

**6** Copy and complete the sentence.

Digesting food is a _____ change.

**7** Look at the pictures. Then copy and complete the sentences.

Combing your hair is a _____ change.
Growing your hair is a _____ change.

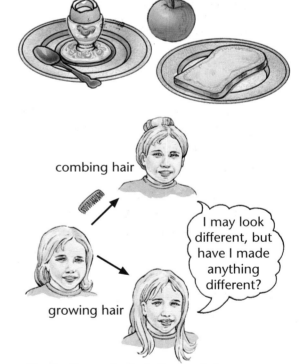

combing hair

I may look different, but have I made anything different?

growing hair

*Our bodies make hair from substances we eat in our food.*

**WHAT YOU NEED TO REMEMBER** (Copy and complete using the **key words**)

**Chemical changes**

Chemical changes always make _____ substances.

Life itself involves _____ changes.

**More about changes: C2.1, C2.2**

# 4.2 Acids

We need to drink water to stay alive. But very few people drink pure water. We like lots of different flavours. Some people like lots of sugar in their drinks. Other people prefer a tangier taste.

One thing that many drinks have in common is that they contain <u>acids</u>. Many people seem to like the sour, sharp taste.

**1** Write down a list of drinks that contain acids.

*All these drinks contain acid.*

### ■ Captain Cook's voyage

Captain Cook discovered Australia. He knew that eating fresh fruit would keep his sailors free from a dreadful disease called scurvy. So he made his men eat limes and lemons. During the long voyage of three and a half years, only one sailor died of scurvy. Afterwards, the British Navy made its sailors drink lime juice to keep them healthy.

This is why, even today, British sailors are often called 'Limeys'.

**2** Copy and complete the sentences.

Lime juice tastes _____.
This is because it contains citric _____.
Lime juice prevents scurvy because it contains _____.

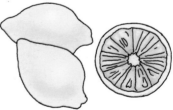

*Limes and lemons taste **sour** because they contain citric acid. They prevent scurvy because they contain vitamin C. This is also an acid, but very weak.*

### ■ Health warning

While many weak acids are harmless, there are other acids that are very powerful. Sulphuric acid is one of these.

Sulphuric acid is too dangerous to use in anything we eat or drink. It is very **corrosive**. The hazard warning sign shows you what this means.

**3** What <u>two</u> things does the hazard warning sign tell you?

**CORROSIVE**

**4 (a)** Explain why you should <u>not</u> get sulphuric acid on your skin.

**(b)** Explain why you should <u>never</u> taste sulphuric acid.

**5** Not all acids are as dangerous as sulphuric acid. Write down the names of two acids that are not dangerous. (Hint: remember the limes.)

### DID YOU KNOW?

In 1949 a man called Haigh became known as the Acid Bath Murderer. He got rid of the people he had killed by putting their bodies in a bath filled with concentrated sulphuric acid. The police searched where Haigh had dumped the sludge from the bath. They found some bone, false teeth and three gallstones. This was enough evidence to convict Haigh.

### ■ Do acids dissolve everything?

In days gone by, a man tried to swindle a very wise king. He held up a bottle of a liquid and said:

'Your majesty, in this bottle I have a corrosive acid that will dissolve anything and everything.'

The king called for his guards and had the man thrown into prison.

**6** How did the king know that the man was lying?

**7 (a)** What do we keep laboratory acids in?

**(b)** What does this tell us about these acids and glass?

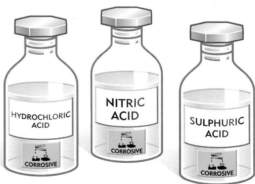

### WHAT YOU NEED TO REMEMBER (Copy and complete using the **key words**)

**Acids**

Acids are substances that taste _____.

Some acids, like sulphuric acid, are dangerous because they are _____.

You should <u>never</u> taste laboratory acids.

**More about acids: C3.5**

# 4.3 How can we tell whether something is an acid?

When acids are dissolved in water, they look just like water. You could tell they are acids by tasting them. Anything that tastes sour is an acid. But many acids are too dangerous to taste.

1  Why can't you tell a liquid is an acid just by looking at it?

2  Why shouldn't we taste substances to see whether they are acids?

## ■ Using litmus to test for acids

We can use special **dyes** to check for acids. These dyes are called <u>indicators</u> because they change **colour** and indicate (tell us) whether the substance is an acid.

Litmus is a well-known indicator.

3  (a)  What colour is litmus on its own?

   (b)  What colour is litmus when it is in acid?

4  Copy the table. Either shade each space in the litmus colour or write in the name of the colour.

A substance that turns litmus blue is called an <u>alkali</u>. Alkalis are the opposites of acids.

A substance that is neither an acid nor an alkali is <u>neutral</u>. Litmus does not change colour in neutral substances.

5  Look at the table again.

   (a)  Which one of the substances is neutral?

   (b)  Which three substances are alkalis?

6  Look at the bottles of alkalis. Copy and complete the sentences.

Alkalis have names that end in _____.
Like acids, alkalis are _____.

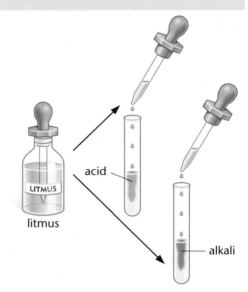

| Substance | Turns litmus this colour |
|---|---|
| sodium hydroxide | blue |
| vitamin C | red |
| water | purple |
| calcium hydroxide | blue |
| carbon dioxide | red |
| hydrochloric acid | red |
| potassium hydroxide | blue |

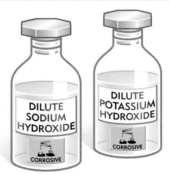

*Sodium hydroxide and potassium hydroxide are alkalis. Like acids they are corrosive.*

## Universal indicator

Litmus has only three different colours. So it can only tell you if something is acidic, alkaline or neutral. It can't tell you that sulphuric acid is more acidic than lemon juice.

Universal indicator has all the colours of the rainbow. So it can tell you how strong an acid or an alkali is.

7 Copy out the table, but put the most acidic liquid first and the least acidic last.

## The acidity scale

We use a special scale of acidity called the **pH** scale. (Say the letters 'pea–aitch'.)

- Acids have pH numbers **less** than 7.
- Alkalis have pH numbers **more** than 7.
- Neutral substances have a pH **equal** to 7.

8 (a) Which is more acidic, pH = 2 or pH = 6?

(b) Which is more alkaline, pH = 8 or pH = 11?

## Using universal indicator to measure pH

Each colour in the universal indicator range has its own pH number.

9 Write the correct pH number by each liquid in your answer to question 7.

more acidic — neutral — more alkaline

*Universal indicator turns different colours according to how acidic or alkaline a substance is.*

A B C D

| Liquid | Colour with universal indicator |
|--------|-------------------------------|
| A | green |
| B | yellow |
| C | red |
| D | orange |

| 0 | 1 | 2 | 3 | 4 | 5 | 6 | 7 | 8 | 9 | 10 | 11 | 12 | 13 | 14 |

more acidic — neutral — more alkaline

*The pH scale.*

red  orange  yellow  green  blue  navy blue  purple

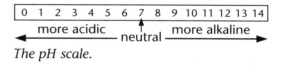

| 0–2 | 3–4 | 5–6 | 7 | 8–9 | 10–12 | 13–14 |

more acidic — neutral — more alkaline

---

**WHAT YOU NEED TO REMEMBER** (Copy and complete using the **key words**)

**How can we tell whether something is an acid?**

Indicators are special _____. They change _____ when mixed with acids or alkalis.

Universal indicator helps us to measure a substance's _____.

Alkalis have a pH of _____ than 7.
Acids have a pH of _____ than 7.
Neutral substances have a pH _____ to 7.

**More about acids: C3.5**

# 4.4 Getting rid of an acid with an alkali

Chemists are a bit like magicians! They can't make rabbits disappear or turn them into carrots, but they <u>can</u> change things!

If you put one drop of hydrochloric acid on a glass slide then add one drop of sodium hydroxide, a bit of chemical magic takes place. The acid and the alkali react together to make salt – exactly the same salt that you put on food! The proper name for this salt is <u>sodium chloride</u>.

**1** How do you know that adding sodium hydroxide to hydrochloric acid is a chemical change?

**2** What <u>two</u> new substances does this reaction make?

**REMEMBER** from page 58

In chemical reactions new substances are made.

*If you add just the right amount of alkali to an acid, you can make the acid disappear.*

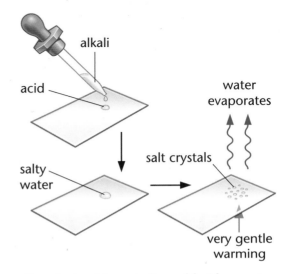

*hydrochloric acid + sodium hydroxide → sodium chloride + water*

## ■ How do you know how much alkali to add to the acid?

Things are not as simple as the first experiment suggested.

If you don't add enough alkali, you get some acid left.

If you add too much alkali, you get some alkali left.

When just the right amount of alkali is added to the acid, there is no acid or alkali left over.

The solution is <u>neutral</u>, so this kind of chemical reaction is called **neutralisation**.

**3** Why is the chef's way of solving this problem not a good idea?

IT STILL DOESN'T TASTE QUITE RIGHT!

*NEVER do this to check whether the acid has gone.*

## ■ Neutralisation

We need to know exactly how much alkali we should add to the acid to make a perfectly neutral solution. We can't just guess, so we use an **indicator** to tell us.

Susan puts some acid in a test-tube. She adds a few drops of litmus indicator. Susan then uses a dropper to slowly add an alkali to the acid.

4 **(a)** At which point – A, B or C – has the alkali just neutralised the acid?

**(b)** Susan wants some salt. Which is the best solution to evaporate?

If we add the acid to the alkali, we still get the same neutralisation reaction.

5 Copy the diagram. Colour solution Z correctly.

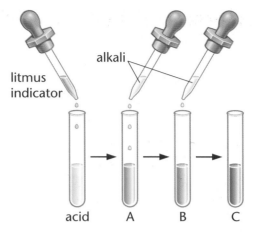

*Adding alkali to acid.*

## ■ Can we use other acids and alkalis?

If we use a different acid or a different alkali, they will still neutralise each other.
One of the new substances produced is always **water**.
The other new substance is still called a **salt** but it is <u>different</u> from ordinary salt (sodium cloride).

We can use potassium hydroxide instead of sodium hydroxide to neutralise hydrochloric acid.

6 What salt do we now get?

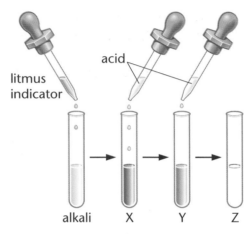

*Adding acid to alkali.*

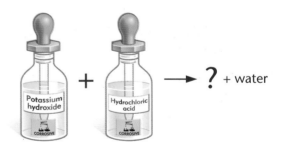

*potassium hydroxide + hydrochloric acid → potassium chloride + water*

---

**WHAT YOU NEED TO REMEMBER** (Copy and complete using the **key words**)

**Getting rid of an acid with an alkali**

When we mix an alkali with an acid, we get a reaction called _____.

Neutralisation reactions make two new substances, a _____ and _____.

To help us know when neutralisation is complete, we use an _____.

**More about neutralisation: C3.6**

# 4.5 Using neutralisation reactions

Neutralisation reactions, where acid and alkali react together, don't just happen in test-tubes. They are very important in our daily lives.

**REMEMBER** from pages 63 and 65

pH 0 1 2 3 4 5 6   7   8 9 10 11 12 13 14
← more acidic      more alkaline →

When we mix an acid with an **alkali**, they neutralise each other.

### Keeping your teeth healthy

Your mouth is full of bacteria. These feed on sugar from left-over food. Whenever bacteria eat sugar, they make acid. Acid then attacks your teeth.

When you brush your teeth, you remove bits of food and the bacteria.

Toothpaste also contains substances that neutralise the acid that rots your teeth. For example, some toothpastes contain bicarbonate of soda.

1  (a)  Is toothpaste slightly alkaline, neutral or acidic?

   (b)  Why is this useful?

   (c)  Name a substance that is put into toothpaste to give it a pH of more than 7.

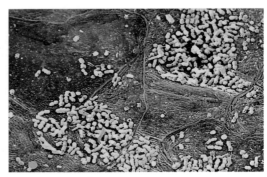

*Bacteria on a human tongue.*

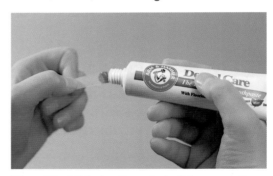

*The pH of this toothpaste is 8 because it contains bicarbonate of soda.*

### Curing upset stomachs

Too much acid in the stomach causes indigestion. Some people take medicines to neutralise the stomach acid.

2  Milk of Magnesia indigestion tablets contain magnesium hydroxide. This is a very weak alkali. Why couldn't the tablets contain sodium hydroxide?

3  How do medicines like Milk of Magnesia cure indigestion?

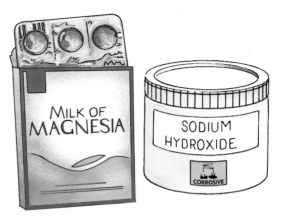

*One of these is a medicine for indigestion.*

Other indigestion cures contain magnesium **carbonate** or bicarbonate of soda. These neutralise acids but also make a gas called **carbon dioxide**.

**4** Both magnesium carbonate and bicarbonate of soda make people burp. Why is this?

## ■ Baking a cake

Some cake recipes use baking powder. This contains bicarbonate of soda and crystals of a weak acid. When you make them wet, the acid and the bicarbonate of soda neutralise each other.

The reaction gives off carbon dioxide gas.

**5** How does baking powder make the cake rise?

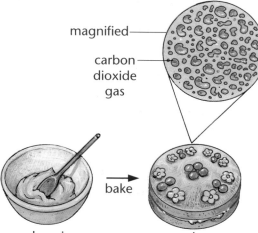

magnified

carbon dioxide gas

bake

cake mix          cake

*Trapped carbon dioxide gas makes the cake rise.*

## ■ Neutralising acidic lakes

Scandinavian countries add crushed limestone to their lakes to neutralise the acidity that comes from acid rain.

Limestone is calcium carbonate. This neutralises acids and gives off carbon dioxide gas. Other carbonates and bicarbonates react with acid in the same way.

**6** What would you see happen when the limestone is added to the acidic lake?

**WHAT YOU NEED TO REMEMBER** (Copy and complete using the **key words**)

**Using neutralisation reactions**

We can neutralise an acid with an _____.

We can also neutralise acids by using sodium bicarbonate or a _____. These react with the acid to give the gas _____ _____.

**More about neutralisation: C3.6**

# 4.6 How do metals react with acids?

We know that when sugar dissolves in water, nothing new is made. Although the sugar seems to disappear, it is still in the water.

1 How could you prove that the sugar is still in the water?

2 Is dissolving sugar in water a chemical or physical change? Explain your answer.

## ■ What happens when magnesium reacts with an acid?

Look at the picture. The acid does not just dissolve the magnesium. It <u>reacts</u> with the magnesium. Two new substances are made.

3 What two new substances are made?

4 Copy and complete the sentence.

Because adding magnesium to dilute hydrochloric acid makes new substances, it is a _____ change.

5 Which one of these two sentences is the more accurate? Copy it down.

- The magnesium dissolves in the acid.
- The magnesium reacts with the acid.

## ■ Investigating the gas made in the reaction

If we test the gas with a lighted splint, we get a 'pop'. This is the chemical test for hydrogen.

6 Is this test for hydrogen a chemical or a physical change? Explain your answer.

> **REMEMBER** from pages 25 and 58
>
> In a physical change, no new substances are made.
>
> In a chemical change, new substances are made.

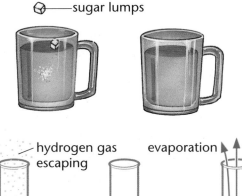
sugar lumps

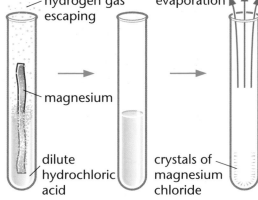
hydrogen gas escaping
magnesium
dilute hydrochloric acid
evaporation
crystals of magnesium chloride

*We can write down what happens in the reaction like this:*
*magnesium + hydrochloric acid → magnesium chloride + hydrogen*

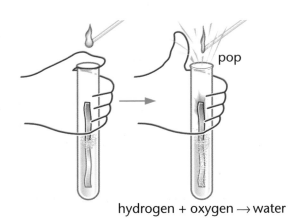
pop

hydrogen + oxygen → water

When magnesium reacts with the acid, the metal pushes **hydrogen** out of the acid.

We can collect the hydrogen gas in a balloon and let it go. With a little luck, the balloon might go as far as ten miles or so!

**7** Write as much as you can about hydrogen gas, from the information on this page and page 68.

*The balloon will rise up in the air. You can put your school address in a plastic bag and see where it goes.*

### ■ Separating the salt made in the reaction

The other new material that is made when magnesium reacts with hydrochloric acid is a **salt**.

We make sure that all the acid is used up by using more magnesium than we need. The reaction has finished when there are no more bubbles of hydrogen produced.

We then filter off the left-over magnesium.

The diagrams show how you can get crystals of the salt that was made in the reaction.

**8** Write down the following sentences in the correct order.

- Wait till there are no more bubbles of hydrogen.

- Cool and wait for crystals to grow.

- Add magnesium to the acid.

- Filter off the left-over magnesium.

- Boil off about half of the water.

**9** Copy and complete.

When magnesium reacts with hydrochloric acid you get a salt called _____ _____.

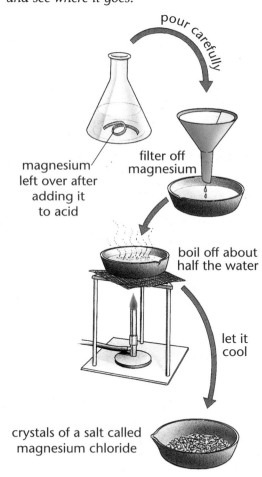

pour carefully

magnesium left over after adding it to acid

filter off magnesium

boil off about half the water

let it cool

crystals of a salt called magnesium chloride

---

**WHAT YOU NEED TO REMEMBER** (Copy and complete using the **key words**)

**How do metals react with acids?**

Metals react with dilute acids to make a _____.

Metals push _____ out of the acid.

**More about metals and acids: C2.6**

# 4.7 Salt and salts

Salt is a very important substance. We put salt on our food. We also use salt to make lots of other useful chemicals.

**1** Write down two ways of getting salt.

When we say or write the word **salt** in everyday life, what we usually mean is 'common salt'. Its chemical name is sodium chloride. This tells us that it is made of two simple substances that are called <u>elements</u>.

**2** What two elements make common salt?

■ **Looking at salt under a magnifying glass**

Look at the picture of salt.

**3** Copy and complete each sentence. Use the best describing word from each group.

**(a)** Salt is made up of _____.
drops / crystals / bits / specks

**(b)** Each crystal is shaped like a _____.
triangle / circle / cube / ball

**(c)** Salt looks white but each crystal is really
_____.
red / blue / colourless / black

■ **Looking at other salts**

Sodium chloride is not the only salt. There are **hundreds** of different salts. Most of them dissolve in **water**.

Salts usually contain a metal element joined with at least one **non-metal** element.

The first name of the salt is that of the metal. The second name tells you the non-metal.

A salt mine in Cheshire.

Salt from the Australian seas. In hot dry places, people get salt by letting sea water evaporate.

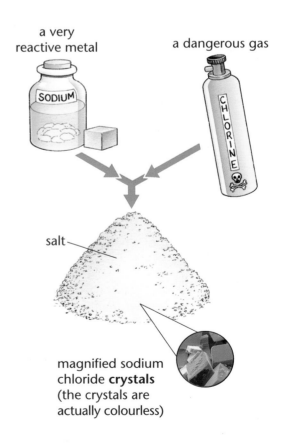

a very reactive metal

SODIUM

a dangerous gas

CHLORINE

salt

magnified sodium chloride **crystals** (the crystals are actually colourless)

## Potassium chloride

This looks and tastes like sodium chloride.

4 (a) Write down what crystals of potassium chloride look like.

 (b) Write down the metal element and non-metal element that make this salt.

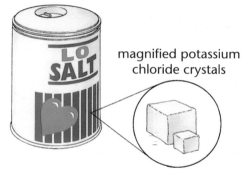

magnified potassium chloride crystals

*Too much sodium in your diet can be bad for you. Lo Salt contains twice as much potassium chloride as sodium chloride.*

## Magnesium sulphate

This is made up of the metal element magnesium. The sulphate part of the salt contains the non-metal elements sulphur and oxygen.

5 What are the three elements in magnesium sulphate?

6 Do you think that magnesium sulphate is harmful? Explain your answer.

*Magnesium sulphate is added to make it easier to float in this flotation bath.*

## Copper sulphate

Nearly all the salts of the metal copper are either green or blue.

7 Write down what crystals of copper sulphate look like.

8 What are the three elements that make up copper sulphate?

*Copper sulphate.*

## WHAT YOU NEED TO REMEMBER (Copy and complete using the **key words**)

**Salt and salts**

We know sodium chloride as common _____.

There are _____ of different salts.

A salt usually contains a metal element joined to at least one _____.

Salts form _____.

Most salts dissolve in _____.

**More about metals and acids: C2.6**

# 4.8 Other kinds of chemical reaction

## Oxidation reactions

Oxygen joins on to many other elements. We say that oxygen oxidises other elements. We call these reactions **oxidation** reactions.

Some oxidation reactions are a big problem. Other oxidation reactions are very useful.

## Rusting – a big problem

Oxygen from the air can react with iron.

1 Look at the diagram. Then copy and complete the following.

Both _____ and _____ must be present for rusting to take place.

Rusting is an _____ reaction.

## Combustion – a big help

Burning is a chemical reaction. The elements in the burning substances join with oxygen from the air. Heat and light energy are given out as flames.

Another word for burning is **combustion**.

All combustion reactions involve oxidation.

2 (a) What is burned in the motorbike?

(b) Where does this reaction take place?

(c) What else is needed for this to happen?

## Respiration – the life giver

The food we eat helps us to keep warm and to move. The oxygen we breathe joins on to carbon and hydrogen in our food, and releases energy. This is an oxidation reaction called <u>respiration</u>. It is not burning or combustion because there are no flames inside your body.

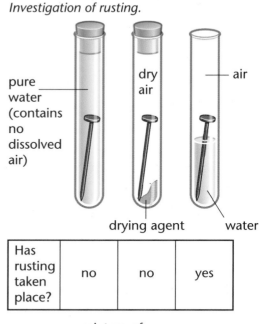

*Investigation of rusting.*

pure water (contains no dissolved air) — dry air — air — drying agent — water

| Has rusting taken place? | no | no | yes |
|---|---|---|---|

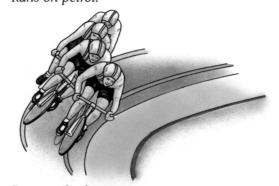

mixture of petrol and air

engine cylinder

*Runs on petrol.*

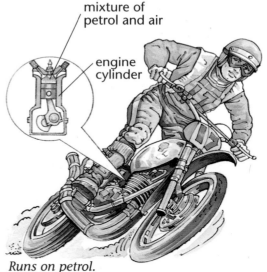

*Runs on food.*

**3** Copy and complete the sentences using these words: combustion, oxidation, respiration

The cyclist releases energy by _____.

The motorbike releases energy by _____.

Both are _____ reactions.

## ■ Test for oxygen

Look at the picture of the test for oxygen gas.

**4** Which <u>two</u> of the following best describe the reaction which happens in the test?

rusting, oxidation, respiration, combustion

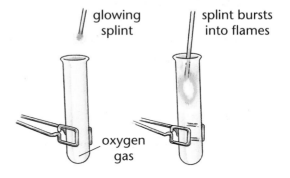

glowing splint

splint bursts into flames

oxygen gas

*Test for oxygen.*

## ■ Decomposition

Not all reactions involve elements <u>joining</u> together. Many reactions are like the one shown in the picture.

We can <u>break down</u> complicated substances into simpler ones. This breakdown is called **decomposition**. If we need heat to break a substance down, we call the reaction a <u>thermal</u> decomposition.

**5** Look at the picture.

(a) Which substance is being decomposed?

(b) Write down the name of one of the substances it splits up into.

**6** How does the teacher show that oxygen is given off when potassium nitrate is heated?

safety goggles or visor

Oxygen gas is given off.

glowing splint

molten potassium nitrate

*Thermal decomposition.*

**WHAT YOU NEED TO REMEMBER** (Copy and complete using the **key words**)

**Other kinds of chemical reaction**

A chemical reaction that joins oxygen to a substance is called _____.

Examples of oxidation are rusting, respiration and _____.

If we heat a substance and it breaks down, we call this thermal _____.

**More about chemical reactions: C2.2**

# 4.9 Writing down chemical reactions

Hydrogen reacts with oxygen to make water.

Here is a quick way to write down what happens in this chemical reaction:

hydrogen + oxygen → water

the arrow means
'react to make'

This is called a word **equation**.

We always write word equations in the same way.

On the **left** we put what we <u>start</u> with.

On the **right** we put the **new** substance that we <u>finish</u> with.

1  Copy the diagram and put the following labels in the correct boxes:

finishing substance, starting substance

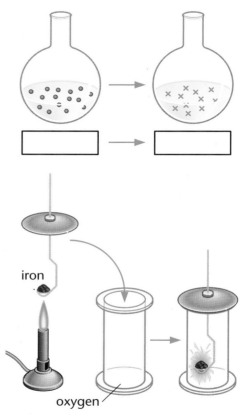

■  **Remember burning?**

Jim burns some iron filings in oxygen.

He starts with iron and oxygen. He finishes up with iron oxide.

The word equation is

iron + oxygen → iron oxide

*Iron burns in oxygen to make iron oxide.*

2  **(a)**  What two substances does this reaction start with?

**(b)**  What substance does this reaction finish with?

Julie burns some magnesium in air. The magnesium reacts with the oxygen contained in the air.

3  Copy and complete the word equation below:

magnesium + _____ → magnesium oxide

*Burning magnesium in air makes magnesium oxide.*

## ■ Naming two-element compounds

Metals can react with non-metals to make new substances. These contain the metal and non-metal joined together. They are called <u>compounds</u>.

We always start the name of the compound with the name of the metal. We write the name of the non-metal last.

Look at the examples. Notice that the name of the non-metal changes slightly.

magnesium + oxygen → magnesium oxide

sodium + chlorine → sodium chloride

iron + sulphur → iron sulphide

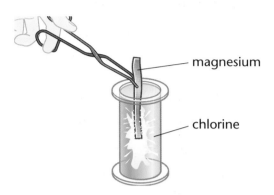

*Magnesium burning in chlorine.*

**4** Write down the name of the compound made by the reaction of:

(a) magnesium + chlorine

(b) copper + sulphur

**5** Copy and complete the word equations.

(a) copper + oxygen → copper _____

(b) _____ + sulphur → iron sulphide

(c) sodium + _____ → _____ chloride

(d) copper + sulphur → _____ _____

(e) _____ + chlorine → copper _____

**6** Iron burns in chlorine.

(a) What compound is formed?

(b) Write a word equation for this reaction.

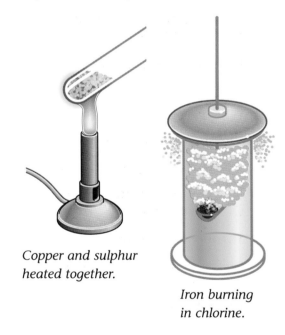

*Copper and sulphur heated together.*

*Iron burning in chlorine.*

---

**WHAT YOU NEED TO REMEMBER** (Copy and complete using the **key words**)

**Writing down chemical reactions**

Chemical reactions make _____ substances.

We show what happens in chemical reactions by writing a word _____.

We put what we start with on the _____.

We put what we finish with on the _____.

**More about reactions: C2.6, C2.7**

# 5.1 Different types of rock

There are hundreds of different types of rock. Some rocks are made from the same substance but they look different. This is because they were made in different ways.

*Limestone is a fairly hard rock made from calcium carbonate.*

*Granite is a very hard rock.*

*Sandstone is a soft rock. You can scratch it with your nails.*

*Chalk is a soft rock made from calcium carbonate. You can rub bits off easily.*

*Marble is a rock made from calcium carbonate crystals. You can smooth and polish it.*

1 Which <u>three</u> rocks are made from the same substance?

2 Which of the rocks would make the best building stone for a castle wall? Give a reason for your answer.

3 Which of the rocks shown can be made into thin tiles that you could use for the roof of a house?

*Slate is a hard rock made of layers. It splits easily into sheets.*

 What types of rocks are used for buildings in the area where you live?

## ■ Some rocks react with acid

Chalk fizzes when acid is dropped on it. This happens because chalk is made from **calcium carbonate**.

4 Copy and complete the sentences.

When acid is dropped on chalk, a gas called _____ _____ is given off. This happens because chalk is made from calcium _____.

5 Which other rocks in the pictures at the top of the page will fizz when acid is added? Give a reason for your answer.

chalk

acid

Carbon dioxide gas is given off.

## Rocks can melt

When rocks get hot enough, they melt and change into a liquid called **magma**. This happens to rock inside the Earth.

6 What is the crust of the Earth made from?

7 What is the name for the hot, molten rock inside the Earth?

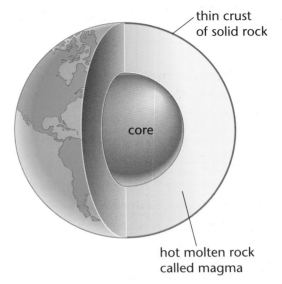

thin crust of solid rock

core

hot molten rock called magma

*Cross-section through the Earth.*

## Molten rock can set hard

Sometimes magma comes up from inside the Earth. This happens when a volcano erupts. When magma cools, it sets hard.

Magma can also cool and set inside the Earth's crust.

8 Look at the diagram.

(a) What is the name of a rock hardened outside the Earth's crust?

(b) What is the name of a rock hardened inside the Earth's crust?

The new rocks that are made when magma sets are called **igneous** rocks.

9 Name two types of igneous rock.

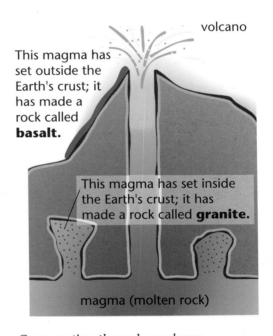

volcano

This magma has set outside the Earth's crust; it has made a rock called **basalt.**

This magma has set inside the Earth's crust; it has made a rock called **granite.**

magma (molten rock)

*Cross-section through a volcano.*

**WHAT YOU NEED TO REMEMBER** (Copy and complete using the **key words**)

**Different types of rock**

Carbon dioxide gas is produced when acid is put on _____ _____.

Hot liquid rock deep in the Earth is called _____.

Rocks made from magma are called _____ rocks.
Examples of igneous rocks are _____ and _____.

**More about different rocks: C3.1**

# 5.2 Getting new rocks from old

There are three ways of getting new rocks from old.

- New rocks are made when molten magma comes up through the Earth's crust and sets hard.

- New rocks are made under the sea from the bits that wear off old rocks.

- Rocks can also be changed into new ones by heat and pressure deep in the Earth's crust.

## ■ Rocks made under the sea

The diagram shows how this happens.

The new rocks are called **sedimentary** rocks.

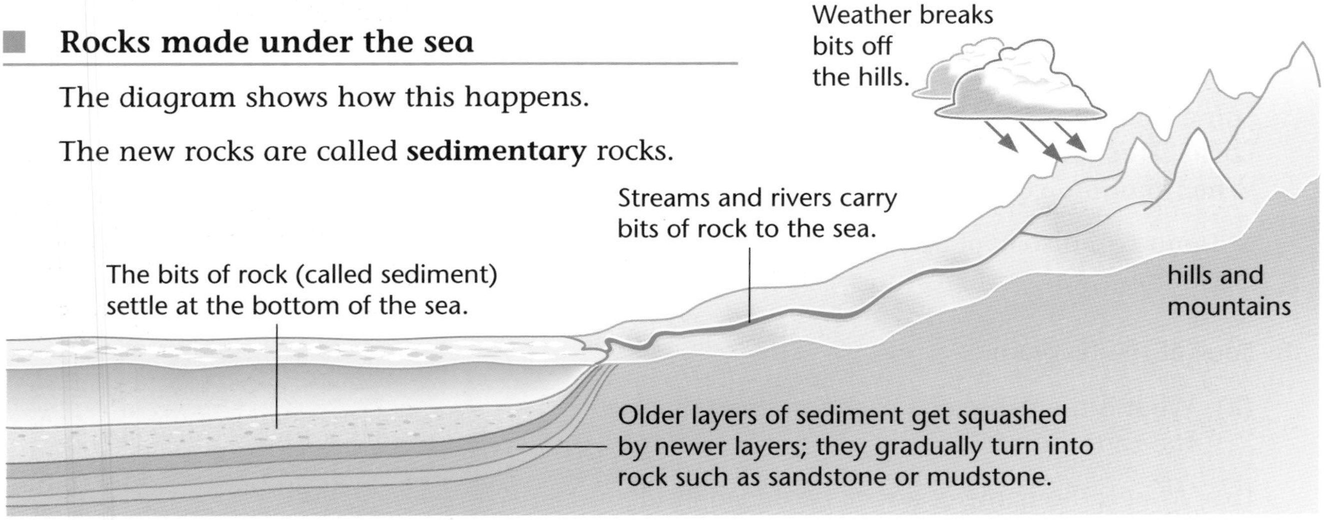

Weather breaks bits off the hills.

Streams and rivers carry bits of rock to the sea.

The bits of rock (called sediment) settle at the bottom of the sea.

hills and mountains

Older layers of sediment get squashed by newer layers; they gradually turn into rock such as sandstone or mudstone.

*How sedimentary rocks are made.*

1 Write down the name of a sedimentary rock.

2 On a copy of the flow chart, write down these words in the correct boxes to tell the story of sedimentary rocks.

- Layers of sediment get squashed as new sediment piles up on top.

- Bits of rock get into streams and rivers.

- The stuff that settles on the sea bed is called sediment.

- Rivers carry pebbles, sand and gravel to the sea.

Bits of rock are broken off hills and mountains by the weather.

▼

▼

▼

The pebbles, sand and gravel from the rivers settle on the sea bed.

▼

▼

▼

Over **millions** of years the bottom layers of sediment stick together to make sedimentary rock.

*The story of sedimentary rocks.*

## ■ Changing rocks with heat and pressure

Marble and limestone look different but they are both the same substance.

**Marble** has been made from limestone by **heat**. Its small grains have been changed into larger crystals. This has been done by heat deep in the Earth's crust.

*Limestone.*      *Marble.*

**Slate** is made from mudstone when it is squashed by the high **pressure** inside the Earth.

*Mudstone.*      *Slate.*

Rocks that are made by changing other kinds of rocks are called **metamorphic** rocks.

**3** How is limestone changed into marble?

**4** How is mudstone changed into slate?

**5** What type of rocks are marble and slate?

**6** Write down:

  **(a)** <u>one</u> way in which limestone and marble are similar.

  **(b)** <u>one</u> way in which limestone and marble are different.

    (Clue: Look back to page 76.)

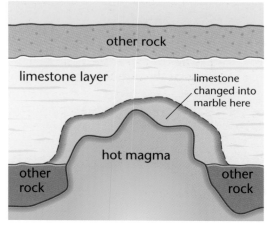

*How limestone is changed to marble.*

**WHAT YOU NEED TO REMEMBER** (Copy and complete using the **key words**)

### Getting new rocks from old

New rocks made under the sea from the bits that wear off the old rocks are called _____ rocks. These rocks are formed over _____ of years.

Rocks can also be made from other rocks by _____ and _____. For example, heat changes limestone into _____, and pressure changes mudstone into _____.

Because marble and slate are both made by changing other rocks, we call them _____ rocks.

**More about different rocks: C3.1**

# 5.3 The rock cycle

Over **millions** of years the substances in the rocks shift round. This gradual shift is called the **rock cycle**.

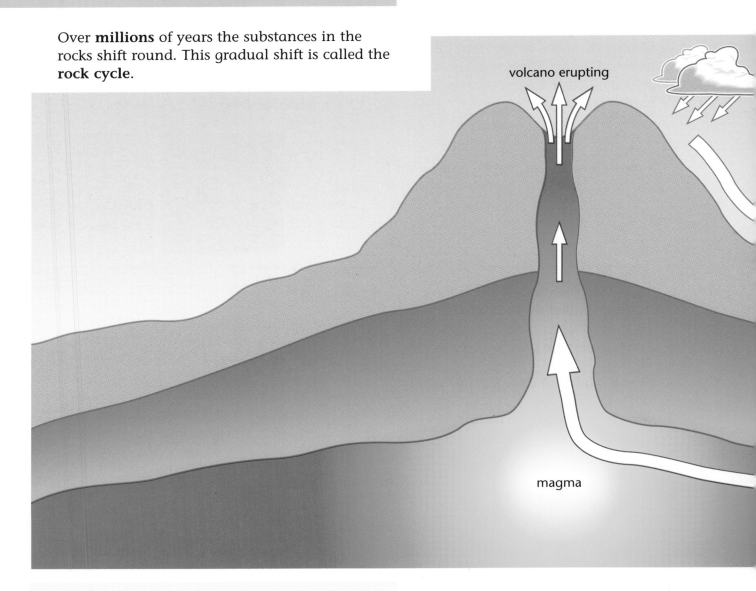

volcano erupting

magma

1 What type of rock is formed when magma cools and goes solid?

2 What breaks tiny pieces off rocks?

3 How do broken bits of rock get to the sea?

4 What is the stuff that settles on the bottom of the sea called?

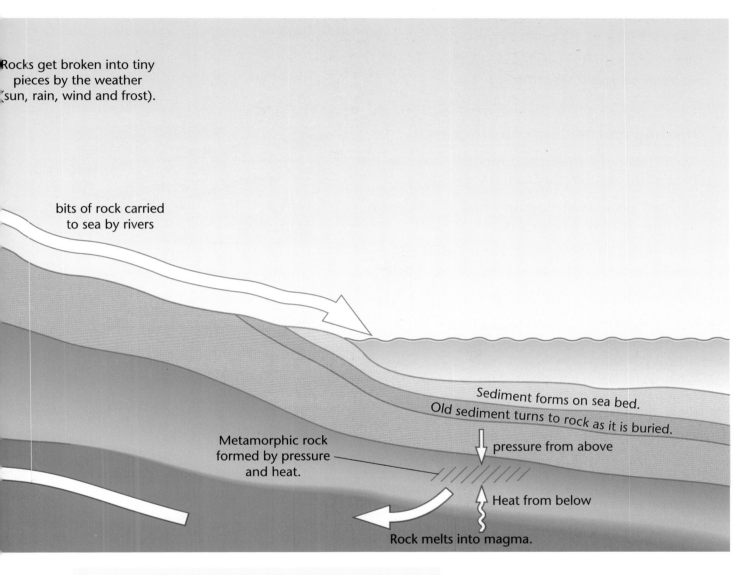

Rocks get broken into tiny pieces by the weather (sun, rain, wind and frost).

bits of rock carried to sea by rivers

Sediment forms on sea bed.
Old sediment turns to rock as it is buried.

pressure from above

Metamorphic rock formed by pressure and heat.

Heat from below

Rock melts into magma.

5  Where are sedimentary rocks formed?

6  What <u>two</u> things can change rock into metamorphic rock?

**WHAT YOU NEED TO REMEMBER** (Copy and complete using the **key words**)

**The rock cycle**

The substances that make up rocks shift around over _____ of years.

We call this shift the _____ _____.

**More about the rock cycle: C3.2**

# 5.4 How the weather breaks up rocks

Hot days, cold nights, rain, frost and wind all help to break up rocks.

When rocks are broken into pieces by the weather we call it **weathering**.

### ■ Heating and cooling can crack rocks

The surface of a rock gets a little bit bigger in the heat of the sun. We say that it <u>expands</u>.

The rock goes smaller again when it cools down at night. We say it <u>contracts</u>.

This constant heating and cooling can make **cracks** in the rock surface. It can even crack a whole rock.

1 What happens to the surface of a rock when it gets hot?

2 What can heating and cooling do to a rock?

3 What else can crack because of heating and cooling?

### ■ Water freezes and cracks rocks

Rain water gets into the cracks. Water **expands** when it freezes. This make the cracks bigger. Sometimes bits of rock **break** off.

4 What happens to water when it freezes?

5 Write the sentences in the correct order to say how water and freezing can break up rocks.

- ■ Bits of rock fall off.
- ■ Water freezes.
- ■ Water gets in the cracks in rocks.
- ■ The cracks in rocks become bigger.

**REMEMBER** from page 78

Rocks get broken up and carried to the sea.

The bits of rock then make new rocks.

*This rock has been cracked by hot days and cold nights in the desert.*

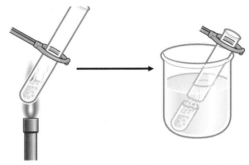

*You should <u>never</u> put a hot test-tube into cold water. If you do, the glass may crack.*

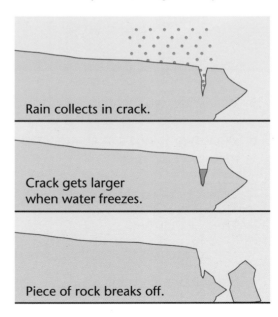

Rain collects in crack.

Crack gets larger when water freezes.

Piece of rock breaks off.

## Two cases of weathering

The weathering of rocks makes varied scenery. A scree slope is made from lots of small pieces of broken rock.

**6** What do you think made the screes at Wastwater?

**7** The weather can also cause problems. Why do you think patched-up holes in the road become holes again in winter?

*The screes at Wastwater in the English Lake District.*

## Wind can cause weathering

Bits of dust and sand blown by the **wind** can wear away rocks or buildings. The pieces are carried away by the wind.

Look at the picture.

**8 (a)** What has happened to parts of the rock?

**(b)** Why has this happened?

**(c)** What is this process called?

*The holes in this rock have been made by sand blown in the wind.*
*This is called **erosion**.*

---

**WHAT YOU NEED TO REMEMBER** (Copy and complete using the **key words**)

**How the weather breaks up rocks**

When rocks are worn away by the weather, we call it _____.

Changes in temperature from hot to cold can make _____ in the surface of a rock. Water gets in cracks and makes them bigger. This happens because water _____ when it freezes.

Sometimes freezing water makes bits of rock _____ off.

Rocks and building materials are also worn away by bits blown in the _____. This is called _____.

**More about weathering: C3.7**

# 5.5 Acids in the air

It isn't just the weather that breaks up rocks. Acid gases in the air also attack rocks.

Look at the grid. It contains 100 x 30 small squares.

The grid shows the main gases in the air.

1 Write down the four main gases in the air.

2 Which gas makes up most of the air?

3 (a) How many small squares are in the grid?

  (b) How many small squares are carbon dioxide?

  (c) Is the amount of carbon dioxide in the air big or small?

The air always contains some **carbon dioxide**. In the last 150 years or so, the amount of carbon dioxide has increased. This is because of all the fuel that we burn.

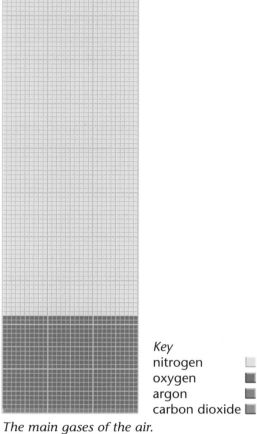

Key
nitrogen
oxygen
argon
carbon dioxide

*The main gases of the air.*

## Making holes in rock

Carbon dioxide dissolves slightly in water and reacts with it to make a very weak **acid**. This weak acid reacts with some rocks like **limestone**, chalk and marble.

Over hundreds of thousands of years, carbon dioxide in rainwater chemically dissolved away large amounts of these rocks. This made caves and caverns.

4 Look at the photograph. What can happen when a lot of limestone gets dissolved away?

*The limestone 'icicles' are called stalactites.*

## Weathering effects on buildings

Some buildings are made from limestone.
So rain containing carbon dioxide very slowly dissolves the outer layer of the stone. It gives the stone a worn look. This is called **chemical** weathering.

5  What causes limestone buildings to look older as the years go by?

## Air pollution

When we burn fuels, we don't just put more carbon dioxide into the air. We also put gases such as sulphur **dioxide** and nitrogen **oxides** into the air. These are much more acidic than carbon dioxide. They cause much **faster** chemical weathering.

Most of the damage to the outsides of ancient buildings has taken place in the last 150 years. From the Industrial Revolution until recently, homes, factories, mills and other industries all burned solid fuel. This produced large amounts of smoke and gases.

6  Why do cathedrals such as York Minster employ teams of stone masons?

7  Which of the photos of York Minster shows newly repaired stonework?

8  Most of the damage to our ancient buildings has taken place during the last 150 years or so. Explain why.

*Stonework on York Minster.*

A

B

### WHAT YOU NEED TO REMEMBER (Copy and complete using the **key words**)

**Acids in the air**

Air contains _____ _____.
This gas dissolves in rain water to make a very weak _____.
This attacks building stone such as _____. We call this process _____ weathering.

When we burn fuels we also make gases such as sulphur _____ and nitrogen _____. These are much more acidic and cause chemical weathering much _____.

**More about acids in the air: C3.7, C3.8**

# 5.6 Things we can do with limestone

Limestone is a very useful rock. The pictures show some of the things we can use it for.

1 Where do we get limestone from?

2 Write down <u>two</u> uses for limestone.

*Limestone quarry.*

*Limestone is used for buildings.*

*Crushed limestone can be spread on fields to make the soil less acidic.*

## ■ Using limestone to make other things

We can use limestone to make other useful materials. To do this we have to use chemical **reactions**.

Limestone is a rock that is made mostly from calcium carbonate.

If you heat limestone strongly you produce a gas called carbon dioxide. The substance left behind is called **calcium oxide**.

Calcium oxide is also called **quicklime**.

3 Copy and complete the sentences.

When calcium carbonate is heated strongly,
_____ _____ gas comes off.
Calcium oxide is left behind.
Calcium oxide is also called _____.
This process takes place in a _____.

*Limestone is heated strongly in a lime-kiln to make quicklime.*

## What is quicklime used for?

We add water to quicklime to make **slaked** lime. We use slaked lime in many different ways, for example in glassmaking and mortar, and to spread on fields.

*Using mortar.*

**4** How is quicklime changed into slaked lime?

**5** Write down <u>three</u> different uses for slaked lime.

## Making lime-water

The other name for slaked lime is **calcium hydroxide**. Calcium hydroxide dissolves slightly in water. The solution is called lime-water.

The diagram shows how to make lime-water.

**6** How can you make lime-water?

## Using lime-water

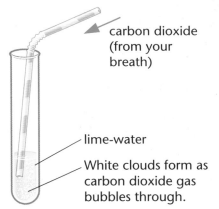

**Carbon dioxide** gas makes lime-water go milky. A reaction happens that makes calcium carbonate. Calcium carbonate does not dissolve in water so it appears as a white cloud of tiny particles.

**7** What gas makes lime-water go milky?

**8** Why does the calcium carbonate appear as a white cloud?

---

### WHAT YOU NEED TO REMEMBER (Copy and complete using the **key words**)

**Things we can do with limestone**

Chemical _____ are used to make useful materials.

If you heat limestone, you make it into a useful substance called _____ _____.
The other name for calcium oxide is _____.

If you add water to quicklime, you get another useful substance called _____ lime.
The other name for slaked lime is _____.

Lime-water is made by dissolving calcium hydroxide in water.
Lime-water turns milky when _____ _____ is bubbled through it.

# 5.7 Getting metals from rocks

The rocks of the Earth's crust often contain metals. For example, we always find gold in lumps or as small bits of metal in the ground. Metals found like this are called **native** metals.

1 Look at the pictures. Write down the names of <u>two</u> other metals that we sometimes find as native metals.

 Find out in which countries are the largest gold mines.

*Native gold.*

*Native silver.*

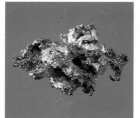

*Native copper.*

## ■ Metal ores

Most metals cannot be found as native metals. They are always joined (combined) with other substances in rocks.

The rocks we get metals from are called **ores**.

2 What is the name for any rock that we get a metal from?

3 What is the name for aluminium ore?

4 Which metal is in rock salt?

5 What is the name for the ore that contains lead joined with sulphur?

6 Copy and complete the table.

| Metal | Ore |
|-------|-----|
| iron | |
| | galena |
| sodium | |
| | bauxite |

*Rock salt is mostly sodium combined with chlorine.*

*Bauxite is an ore that we get aluminium from. It is mainly aluminium combined with oxygen.*

*Galena is an ore that we get lead from. It is mainly lead combined with sulphur.*

*Haematite is an ore that we get iron from. It is mainly iron combined with oxygen.*

### ■ Extracting iron from iron ore

We get **iron** from iron ore by heating the ore with coke in a **blast** furnace. The diagram shows what happens.

**7** What is blown into the blast furnace?

**8** What happens to the iron oxide in the blast furnace?

**9** How do you get the iron out of the blast furnace?

Find out:

(a) when and where iron was first produced using coke;

(b) where coke comes from;

(c) what was used to produce iron from iron ore before that.

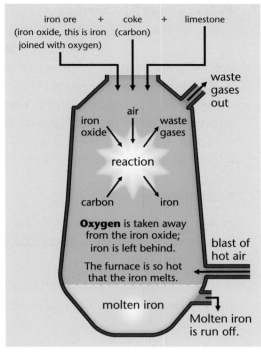

iron ore + coke + limestone
(iron oxide, this is iron (carbon)
joined with oxygen)

waste gases out

iron oxide   air   waste gases

reaction

carbon   iron

**Oxygen** is taken away from the iron oxide; iron is left behind.

The furnace is so hot that the iron melts.

blast of hot air

molten iron

Molten iron is run off.

*Inside a blast furnace.*

### ■ Extracting aluminium from aluminium ore

To get **aluminium** you have to melt aluminium oxide and pass electricity through it. This is called **electrolysis**.

**10** What is the aluminium oxide split up into?

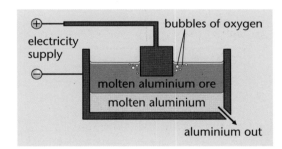

electricity supply

bubbles of oxygen

molten aluminium ore

molten aluminium

aluminium out

---

**WHAT YOU NEED TO REMEMBER** (Copy and complete using the **key words**)

**Getting metals from rocks**

You can find some metals such as gold, silver and copper as lumps in the ground. These are called _____ metals.

Most metals come from rocks called _____.

Iron ore contains oxygen joined with _____.

We get the iron from the ore by taking away the _____. This is done by heating it in a _____ furnace.

We have to use electricity to extract _____ from aluminium oxide. This process is called _____.

**More about getting metals out of rocks: C3.3**

# 5.8 A problem with metals

When metals are new, they are usually bright and shiny. But most metals start to go dull very quickly. This is because they can join with substances from the air. We say that metals **corrode**. Corrosion is a chemical **reaction**.

## Rusting

When iron corrodes, we say that it <u>rusts</u>. Rusting is a chemical reaction. It can damage anything made from iron.

Ann wants to find out what makes iron nails go rusty. The diagrams show what she did.

1 Look at the diagrams. Then copy and complete the table.

| Tube | What's in the tube with the iron nail? | Did it rust? (Yes or No) |
|------|------|------|
| A | Only _____ | No |
| B | Only _____ | _____ |
| C | _____ and _____ | _____ |

2 Copy and complete the sentence.

Iron will only rust when _____ and _____ are present together.

## Protecting iron and steel from rusting

Steel is made mainly from iron. So most steel goes rusty too. Steel is a very useful metal for making things but it has to be protected from rusting.

3 Write down <u>three</u> common uses for steel.

4 Write down <u>three</u> ways in which rusting is prevented.

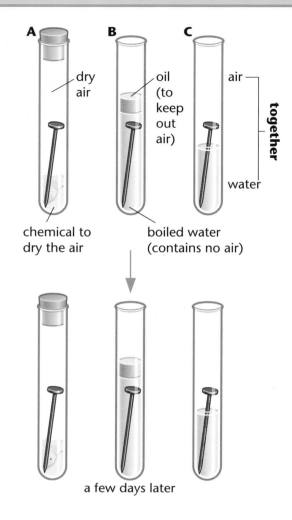

a few days later

Oily bicycle chain.

Tins are made from steel coated with tin.

Galvanised steel screw (steel coated with zinc).

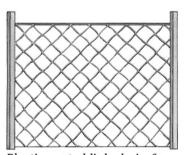

Plastic-coated link-chain fence.

When the bonnet of a car gets hit with a stone, the paint can get chipped. Once the steel starts to rust, the rest of the steel rusts faster.

5 Explain why a rust spot forms where the paint gets chipped.

6 (a) What could you do to prevent a small rust spot from spreading?

(b) What else might you need to do if the rusting is more severe?

*To repair this, you need to sand the rust off down to the shiny metal. You then need to patch the crack and repaint.*

## ■ Bronze statues

Sculptors often make metal statues from bronze. **Bronze** does not rust but it does corrode. This reaction makes the statues go green.

7 Which side of the statue has been cleaned? Give a reason for your answer.

Just as with stone, polluted air attacks **metals** faster than clean air.

8 Where would the statues corrode fastest – in a big city, small town or country village? Explain your answer.

*This statue is being cleaned. They do this by removing the corroded metal on the surface.*

---

**WHAT YOU NEED TO REMEMBER** (Copy and complete using the **key words**)

**A problem with metals**

Rusting is a chemical _____.

Iron only rusts when in both air and water _____.

Metals such as _____ do not rust. But they do _____.

Polluted air causes much faster corrosion of _____.

**More about corrosion: C3.4**

# 5.9 Why do we keep on polluting the air?

We know that polluted air damages stone and makes metals corrode faster. We know that when we burn fuels, we cause pollution.

Fuels must be very important to us if we keep on doing something that is harmful.

## ■ What are fuels and why do we burn them?

A **fuel** is something that we can easily and safely burn. Burning fuels give out **energy**.

1 Look at the drawing. Write down for each letter (A, B, C and D) which fuel is being used. The fuels are:

charcoal, wax, paraffin and gas.

*Burning fuels gives us light and makes things hotter.*

## ■ Exhaust fumes from cars

Cars burn petrol or diesel fuel. Some of the energy is turned into useful movement energy.

But in the car engine, **nitrogen oxides** are made, as well as lots of other harmful gases. The exhaust fumes from cars can make people ill.

2 Why do you think the police officer is wearing a gas mask?

## ■ Poor air quality

Weather forecasters tell us when the air quality is going to be bad.

People with chest problems are told to stay indoors on days when the air quality is poor.

*More people now have difficulty breathing.*

**3** When the air quality is going to be bad, people are asked not to use their cars if at all possible. Why is this?

**4** Why do you think some cities have pollution meters in their city centres?

**5** Most drivers don't want to give up their cars even though they might make people ill. Why do you think this is?

*Air pollution meter.*

## ■ Making electricity

Electricity makes our lives very comfortable.

**6** Write down a list of things in your house that use electricity.

A lot of coal, oil and gas is burned in power stations to make electricity. Unfortunately, these fuels contain small amounts of sulphur. This burns to make sulphur **dioxide**.

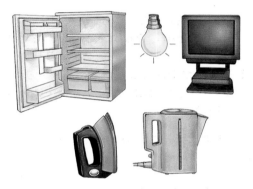

*We can turn the energy of burning fuels into electricity. All these things use electricity.*

Power stations have very tall chimneys. These put the pollution high up in the air. The sulphur dioxide gas dissolves in raindrops to make dilute sulphuric acid or **acid rain**.

The acid rain can come down hundreds of miles away. So it affects the environment of other countries.

**7** What is the effect of acid rain on the Scandinavian lakes and forests?

**8** Why do you think we keep on making acid rain?

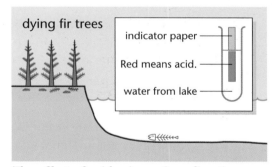

dying fir trees

indicator paper
Red means acid.
water from lake

*The effect of acid rain on Scandinavian lakes and forests.*

## WHAT YOU NEED TO REMEMBER (Copy and complete using the **key words**)

**Why do we keep on polluting the air?**

Something that we can burn easily and safely is called a _____.
When fuels burn, they release _____.

Car engines make harmful gases called _____ _____.

Power stations produce some sulphur _____. This makes _____ _____.

**More about pollution: C3.8**

# C1.1 Using everyday materials

Before we make anything, we should think about what it has to do.

For example, the roof of a house should not be too heavy and should keep out the wind and the rain. So we must cover it with a material that is light in weight, fairly strong and waterproof.

These are the **properties** that the material must have.

The roof of the house in the picture is covered with slates.

1 What properties do you think slate has?

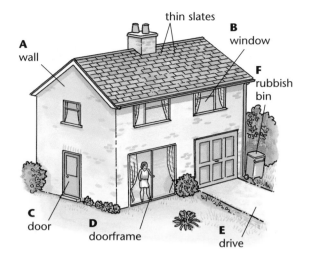

## ■ Other materials used to build a house

Different **materials** have different properties. So we can use them for different **jobs**.

We have to match the properties of the material with the job it has to do.

2 Match each labelled part of the house with a material you could make it from.

Choose from the materials in the table. In some cases there is more than one material you could use.
Set out your answers like this:

**A** wall – brick

3 Now write <u>one</u> sentence saying why you chose each material for each part of the house. Write your sentences like this:

'We can make walls from <u>bricks</u> because <u>they are hard, strong and weatherproof</u>.'

| Material | Properties |
|---|---|
| wood | strong but easily cut into shape |
| glass | transparent |
| brick | hard, strong and weatherproof |
| concrete | can be mixed and poured but sets hard |
| aluminium | easily cut into shape, does not corrode or rot |
| plastic | light, strong, tough and waterproof, does not rot |

## ■ Different materials for different situations

A car is made from many different materials. Each material has the right properties for the job it has to do.

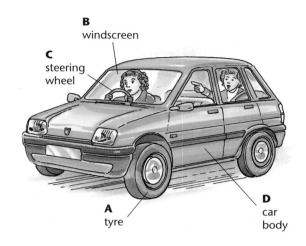

**B** windscreen
**C** steering wheel
**A** tyre
**D** car body

**4 (a)** Write down the materials that are used to make the parts of the car that are labelled on the picture. Choose from:

  steel    plastic    rubber    glass

**(b)** In each case, write down one property of the material that makes it suitable for its job.

## ■ Comparing cars and houses

Cars and houses must let in light and also keep out the rain. But cars must be able to move about and we want houses to last a very long time.

**5** Copy and complete these sentences using the properties in the box.

The windows of a house and the windscreen of a car must be _____ and _____.
But the windscreen of a car must also be _____.

The walls of a house and the body of a car must both be _____ and _____. But the body of the car must not be too _____.

| Some properties of materials |
| --- |
| heavy |
| transparent |
| weatherproof |
| strong |
| shatter-resistant |

**WHAT YOU NEED TO REMEMBER** (Copy and complete using the **key words**)

**Using everyday materials**

We make things from _____.

We use different materials to do different _____.
This is because they have different _____.

**More about materials: CORE+ C1.9, C1.10**

# C1.2 Metals and non-metals

There are more different metallic elements than non-metallic elements. But the Earth's crust is made mainly of elements that are non-metals. Look at the pie chart.

**1 (a)** Which are the two most common elements in the Earth's crust?

**(b)** Are these two elements metals or non-metals?

**(c)** What fraction of the Earth's crust is made up of metallic elements? Is it $\frac{1}{4}$, $\frac{1}{3}$, $\frac{1}{2}$ or $\frac{3}{4}$?

## ■ Metal or non-metal?

We can decide whether an element is a metal or a non-metal by looking at its properties.

> **REMEMBER** from pages 42 and 44
>
> **Metals** are usually:
> - solid at ordinary temperatures;
> - shiny;
> - hard;
> - heavy;
> - strong;
> - tough;
> - easily shaped;
> - conductors of thermal energy;
> - conductors of **electricity**.
>
> **Non-metals:**
> - may be solid, liquid or gas at ordinary temperatures;
> - do not **conduct** heat (thermal energy);
> - do not usually conduct electricity.
>
> Non-metal solids are brittle.

**2** For each of the three elements in the drawings say whether the element is a metal or a non-metal. Give a reason for your choice.

**(a)** chlorine    **(b)** gold    **(c)** iodine

> **REMEMBER** from page 34
>
> Elements are simple substances. All other substances are made from elements joined together in different ways. In nature, there are about 90 different elements.

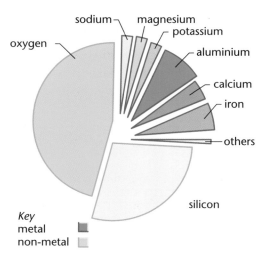

*Elements in the Earth's crust.*

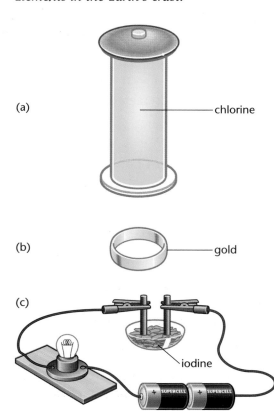

## Why metals are so useful

Metals have many useful properties. So we use them to make many things.

3 Look at the drawings of the nail and the electrical cable. Write down <u>two</u> properties of steel and <u>two</u> properties of copper which make them suitable for these jobs.

[The 'Remember' box on the opposite page may help you.]

The insides of wires are made of copper.

A nail is made of steel.

## Making metals more useful

We can mix metals together to get the properties we want. We call a mixture of metals an <u>alloy</u>.

4 (a) What two elements are mixed to make bronze?

(b) Why do you think the helmet was made from bronze rather than copper?

*This bronze helmet was made from copper mixed with a little tin to give a much harder metal.*

 Find out which alloys are used to make British coins.
What properties must these alloys have?

## Carbon – a very useful non-metal

There are two forms of the element carbon: diamond and graphite. While diamonds are expensive, graphite is cheap.

5 (a) Why are diamonds used as tips for some drills?

(b) Why is graphite used in pencils?

6 Which do you think is more common, diamond or graphite? Give a reason for your answer.

*Diamond is the hardest natural substance.*

*It is millions of times harder than the graphite in a pencil.*

---

**WHAT YOU NEED TO REMEMBER** (Copy and complete using the **key words**)

**Metals and non-metals**

Most of the elements are _____.

All metals are good conductors of heat and _____, but most non-metals do not _____ heat or electricity.

Elements which are gases at room temperature are all _____.

# C1.3  Solids, liquids and gases

There are millions of different materials. But we can put them all into a small number of groups by looking at their properties.

One way of classifying materials is to say whether something is a <u>solid</u>, a <u>liquid</u> or a <u>gas</u>. These are called the <u>three states of matter</u>.

1  Look at the picture. Then write down the name of <u>one</u> solid, <u>one</u> liquid and <u>one</u> gas.

## ■ Solids

Solids stay the same <u>shape</u>.

Unless it gets hotter or colder, a solid also stays the same size. It takes up the same amount of space. We say that its **volume** stays the same.

2  The diamonds in the photograph have been part of the Crown Jewels for about 100 years. The hooks are fixed on to hold the diamonds in place. Explain why they are as easy to put in place now as they were when they were first made.

*These diamonds were cut from the largest diamond ever found. (They are shown smaller than they are in real life.)*

## ■ Liquids

You can pour a liquid from one container to another. So liquids do <u>not</u> have a **shape** of their own. They fill up the container from the bottom and take on its shape.

But liquids do stay the same volume unless they get hotter or colder.

3  (a)  Describe how the shape of the liquid changes when it is poured into the different containers shown in the drawing. Use the words 'ball-shaped', 'tube-shaped', and 'cubic'.

   (b)  What happens to the volume of the liquid as it is poured into the different containers?

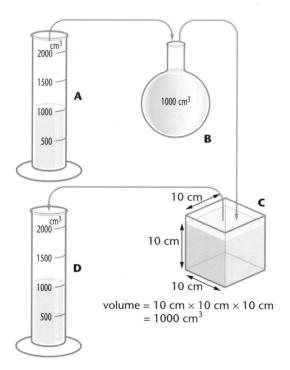

volume = 10 cm × 10 cm × 10 cm
     = 1000 cm³

## ■ Gases

Like a liquid, a gas does not have its own shape. But a gas is different from a liquid because it spreads out into all the **space** in the container.

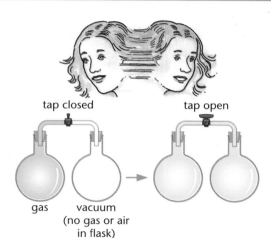

tap closed          tap open

gas     vacuum
(no gas or air
in flask)

4  Look at the diagrams. How do we know that the brown gas spreads out to fill all the space when the tap is opened?

## ■ Other ways of telling them apart

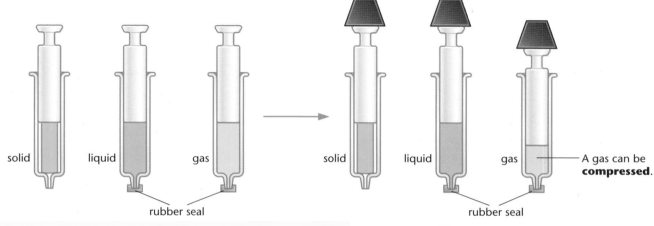

solid        liquid        gas                    solid        liquid        gas        A gas can be
                                                                                         **compressed**.

rubber seal                                              rubber seal

5  Look at the drawings.

   **(a)** Write down another way in which a gas is different from a solid or a liquid.

   **(b)** Look at the gas and water taps. Write down <u>one</u> way in which a gas and a liquid are alike but different from a solid.

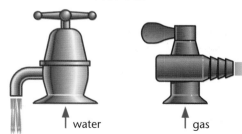

water        gas

Liquids and gases can **flow**.

---

**WHAT YOU NEED TO REMEMBER** (Copy and complete using the **key words**)

**Solids, liquids and gases**

A solid has its own shape and _____.

A liquid has its own volume but not its own _____.

A gas does not have either its own shape or its own volume. It spreads out to fill all the _____ it can.

A gas can be _____.

Liquids and gases can _____.

**More about gases: CORE+ C1.10**

# C1.4  Making models of matter

A model is similar to the real thing in some ways. But it is different in other ways.

In science, we use models to help us understand how things are.

1  Look at the pictures.

   **(a)** Write down <u>one</u> way that the model aircraft is the same as the real aircraft.

   **(b)** Write down <u>two</u> differences between the model and the real one.

**REMEMBER** from pages 14 and 15

Scientists think that solids, liquids and gases are all made of very tiny **particles**.

We can make models of solids and liquids. We do this using particles which are big enough to see.

*This scale model of Concorde:*
- *is exactly the same shape;*
- *is 100 times shorter;*
- *weighs a million times less.*

■ **A model of a solid**

The particles in a solid are held together by strong <u>forces</u>. The particles cannot change places. So solids stay the same **shape** and you can't squash them into a smaller space.

2  Look at the model of the solid.

   **(a)** Write down <u>two</u> ways that the model is similar to a real solid.

   **(b)** Write down <u>two</u> differences between the model and a real solid.

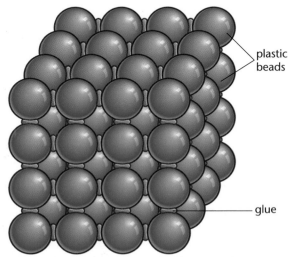

plastic beads

glue

*A model of a solid made from plastic beads and glue. The glue holds the beads in position. The beads are billions of times bigger than the particles in a real solid.*

## A model of a liquid

The particles of a liquid are close together but they can **move** around each other. That means a liquid can flow.

3 **(a)** What happens to the plastic beads in the model liquid when you pour them into the funnel?

**(b)** Why does this happen?

4 Why can't you pour a solid?

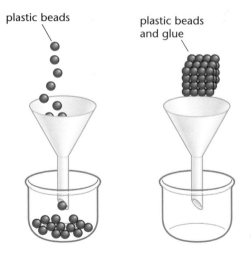

*A model of a liquid.   Can you pour a solid?*

## A model of a gas

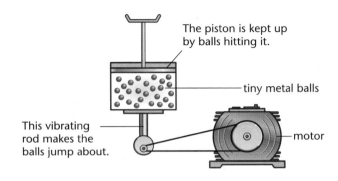

*A model of a gas.*

A gas is made of tiny particles flying about in all directions.

There is lots of **space** in a gas so you can compress it into a smaller volume.

The diagrams show a model of what a gas is like.

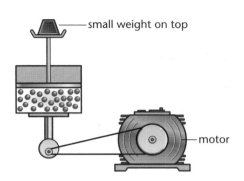

5 **(a)** Write down <u>two</u> ways that the model is like a real gas.

**(b)** Write down <u>two</u> differences between the model gas and a real gas.

**WHAT YOU NEED TO REMEMBER** (Copy and complete using the **key words**)

**Making models of matter**

Solids have their own _____ because the particles cannot move around.
Liquids and gases flow because their particles can _____ around each other.

You cannot squash liquids and solids easily because there is no space between their _____.
You can compress a gas because there is _____ between the particles.

**More about models of matter: CORE+ C1.11 to C1.15**

# C1.5 Getting warmer, getting colder

Solids and liquids stay the same volume if we don't let them heat up or cool down.

If we heat them up they get bigger. We say they **expand**. If we cool them down they get smaller. We say they **contract**.

The diagrams show an experiment with a metal bar.

1 Why do you need the roller and pointer in this experiment?

2 What causes the pointer to move:

(a) clockwise?

(b) anti-clockwise?

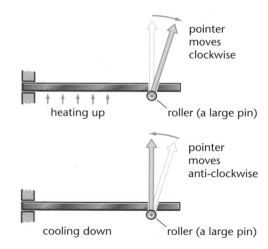

*The length of the metal bar doesn't change very much. The roller and pointer magnify the change so you can see it.*

## ■ Avoiding a problem with expansion

This motorway bridge rests on metal rollers. When the bridge sections expand on hot days, the rollers allow them to move.

3 (a) Why is a gap left between the sections?

(b) What happens to the gap on cold days?

## ■ Using expansion and contraction

When you look at old houses, you sometimes see a metal plate and a big nut and bolt sticking out of the wall. The diagram shows why they are there.

4 Look at the pictures. The walls on the old house are bending. Explain how we can use a tie rod to make them straight again. Use the words <u>expansion</u> and <u>contraction</u> in your answer.

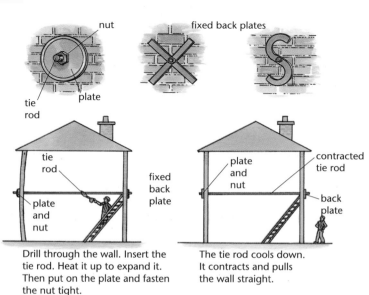

Drill through the wall. Insert the tie rod. Heat it up to expand it. Then put on the plate and fasten the nut tight.

The tie rod cools down. It contracts and pulls the wall straight.

*Before*

*After*

## Expansion and contraction of liquids

If you heat up a liquid, such as mercury, it expands. If you cool down a liquid, it contracts.

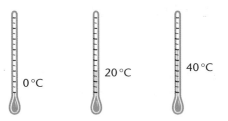

*A mercury-in-glass thermometer.*

**5** Write down the name of a piece of equipment that uses these changes.

**6** Room temperature is usually about 20°C. What happens to the mercury in a thermometer:

**(a)** when the temperature falls to 0°C?

**(b)** when the temperature rises to 40°C?

The hot water system in your home has an expansion pipe. The diagram shows where this is.

**7** What is the expansion pipe for?

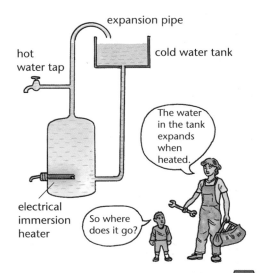

## Heating up a gas

A gas such as air will try to expand when it is heated up.

**8 (a)** What is the volume of air in the syringe at 20°C?

**(b)** What is the volume of the same air at 100°C?

**(c)** What is the increase in volume?

We can stop the air expanding by pushing on the piston of the syringe.

**9** Copy and complete this sentence.

To stop a gas from _____ when it is heated, you must increase the _____.

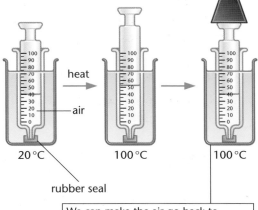

We can make the air go back to 40 cm³ by pressing harder on the gas. We say that we increase the **pressure**.

### WHAT YOU NEED TO REMEMBER (Copy and complete using the **key words**)

**Getting warmer, getting colder**

When we heat solids, liquids or gases, they normally _____.

When solids, liquids and gases cool down, they normally _____.

If we stop a gas expanding when it gets hot, we get an increase in _____.

**More about expansion: CORE+ C1.16**

# C1.6 Mixtures

Sometimes the different things in a mixture are big enough to see. For example, you can see the different things in muesli.

|  | Expensive muesli | Cheap muesli |
|---|---|---|
| nuts | 30% | 5% |
| dried fruit | 35% | 25% |
| oats | 30% | 55% |
| sugar | 5% | 15% |

1 Look at the table. Then copy and complete the sentences.

Cheap muesli contains more _____ and _____ than expensive muesli.

Expensive muesli contains more _____ and _____ than cheap muesli.

A mixture contains different amounts of the things that are mixed. We say that we can mix them in different **proportions**.

■ **Mixing metals**

We often mix metals together to get the properties we want. Look at the diagrams.

2 (a) What metal is gold mixed with?

(b) Why is gold mixed with this metal?

(c) What do we call mixtures of metals?
(Hint: Look back at page 97.)

You can mix gold with different amounts of silver.

3 (a) How much silver is there in 22 carat gold?

(b) Why is 9 carat gold cheaper than 22 carat gold?

■ **Mixing a solid and a liquid**

Tipp-Ex is a mixture of a white solid and a liquid. When you use it, the liquid evaporates. The white solid is left behind on the paper.

4 (a) What happens to the Tipp-Ex in the bottle if you leave it for a while?

(b) Why must you shake the Tipp-Ex before you use it?

*Gold is a very soft metal. We mix it with silver to make it hard.*

22 carat gold contains only a small amount of silver (less than 10%).

9 carat gold contains a lot of silver (more than 60%). This makes it cheaper.

liquid

small marble

specks of white solid

The white solid settles to the bottom.

To mix the white solid and the liquid you must shake the bottle. The marble helps to mix them properly.

## Dissolving a solid in a liquid

The specks in Tipp-Ex are big enough to scatter white light. So the Tipp-Ex looks white.

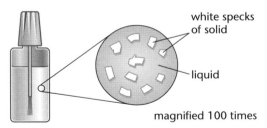

white specks of solid

liquid

magnified 100 times

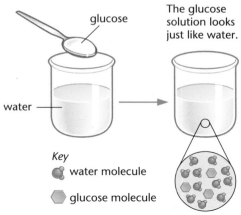

glucose

The glucose solution looks just like water.

water

*Key*

water molecule

glucose molecule

magnified by more than a billion times

But when you mix glucose and water, the glucose seems to disappear. We say that it <u>dissolves</u>.

5 Look at the diagram. Then copy and complete the sentences.

When glucose dissolves in water, glucose _____ are mixed up with water _____.
The glucose seems to disappear because the molecules are too _____ to scatter white light.

6 The glucose solution is made from 1 spoonful of glucose in 200 cm³ of water. Write down <u>two</u> ways that you could you make a weaker glucose solution. (We call a weaker solution 'more dilute'.)

*Water and glucose are both made of* **particles** *(molecules). These molecules are too small to see.*
*When glucose dissolves in water, the glucose molecules are mixed up with the water molecules.*

## A mixture of gases

Air is also a **mixture**. The diagram shows the two main gases in air.

7 What are the main gases in the air?

8 Copy and complete the sentence.

In air there are about 4 molecules of _____ for every molecule of _____.

*Air is a mixture of gases.*

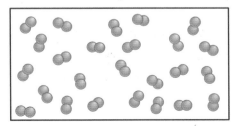

*Key*

molecules of oxygen

molecules of nitrogen

The mixture also contains smaller amounts of argon and carbon dioxide.

---

### WHAT YOU NEED TO REMEMBER (Copy and complete using the **key words**)

**Mixtures**

You can mix things together in different amounts. We say that they can be mixed in different _____.

When you dissolve a solid in a liquid, the _____ of the solid and the liquid get mixed together.

Air is a _____ of gases.

# C1.7 Making pure white sugar

We don't find pure white sugar in the world around us. Sugar is **mixed** up with lots of other things in plants such as sugar cane.

Sugar cane is a special kind of grass. It grows in countries where the weather is hot and damp. Children in these countries love chewing sugar cane because it's got so much sugar in it. But it's also very woody, like bamboo. You certainly wouldn't like sugar cane splinters sprinkled on top of your breakfast cereal!

*Harvesting sugar cane in Cuba.*

## ■ The refining of sugar

The diagrams show how you might **separate** sugar from sugar cane in your school laboratory.

1 Write the following sentences in a sensible order. The first one is already in place.

   Crush the sugar cane.

■ Cool the evaporated juice so that the sugar forms crystals.

■ Mix the crushed sugar cane with water.

■ Separate the sugar crystals from the molasses.

■ Gently evaporate most of the water from the juice.

■ Purify the sugar crystals by re-dissolving in water and re-crystallising.

■ Filter off the wooden bits of cane from the juice.

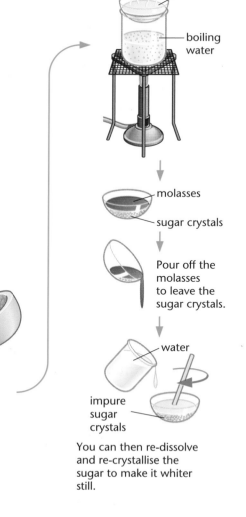

juice

boiling water

molasses

sugar crystals

Pour off the molasses to leave the sugar crystals.

water

impure sugar crystals

You can then re-dissolve and re-crystallise the sugar to make it whiter still.

sugar cane being crushed

The wooden bits do not dissolve in water. They are **insoluble**.

water

The sugar dissolves in water. It is **soluble** in water.

juice

*How to separate sugar from sugar cane.*
*In Cuba this is done in factories.*

## How much sugar dissolves in water?

A lot of sugar will dissolve in a small amount of water. Exactly how much sugar **dissolves** depends upon two things.

- The **more** water we use, then the more sugar dissolves. The graph shows how much sugar dissolves in 100 grams of water.

- The **hotter** the water, the more sugar dissolves. For example, at 20°C, 205 g of sugar dissolves in 100 g of water.

**2 (a)** How much sugar dissolves in 100 g of water at 0°C?

**(b)** How much sugar dissolves in 100 g of water at 80°C?

**(c)** How much sugar would dissolve in 300 g of water at 20°C?

**3** Copy and complete the sentences.

The solubility of sugar is the number of _____ of sugar which will dissolve in 100 g of _____.

As the temperature of the water rises, the solubility of sugar _____.

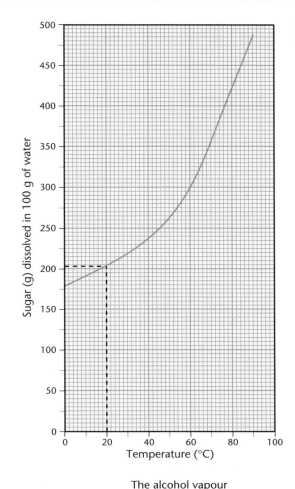

## Using the molasses

Molasses is a black sticky liquid. We sometimes call it black treacle.

Some of the molasses is fermented with yeast. This makes a weak solution of alcohol. The diagram shows how this is made into a stronger drink called rum. This works because alcohol boils off at a lower temperature than water. This process is called <u>fractional distillation</u>.

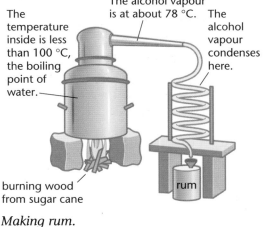

The temperature inside is less than 100 °C, the boiling point of water.

The alcohol vapour is at about 78 °C. The alcohol vapour condenses here.

burning wood from sugar cane

rum

*Making rum.*

---

**WHAT YOU NEED TO REMEMBER** (Copy and complete using the **key words**)

**Making pure white sugar**

We get sugar from plants such as sugar cane. The sugar is _____ up with many other things. To get pure white sugar, we need to _____ it from these other things.
We can do this because sugar _____ in water. We say that it is _____ in water.

We can make more sugar dissolve by using _____ water, or _____ water.

Follows on from: 2.3, 2.4

# C1.8  Separating mixtures

In the world around us, we often find many different substances all mixed up together.

The photographs show some examples of things which are **mixtures** of different substances.

**1** Write down <u>three</u> different things that are mixtures of substances. Try to list some of the substances found in these mixtures.

air

rocks and soil

sea

*Mixtures in the world around us.*

## ■ Pure substances

Sometimes we want to **separate** the different substances in a mixture. We want each substance by itself and not mixed with anything else. We want what we call **pure** substances.

**2** Look at the photographs. Then copy and complete the table.

| Pure substance | What you could get it from |
|---|---|
| oxygen | |
| | sea-water |

 Find out how we can get pure oxygen from the air.

*In hot dry countries, people get pure water from sea-water.*

Pure oxygen is used in hospitals and industry. We get pure oxygen from the air.

## ■ The case of the blackcurrant jelly

Sometimes we just want to find out what substances are in a mixture.

Paula loves jelly but she has to be very careful. She is allergic to E122, a dye used to colour many food items.

The diagram shows how a food scientist could test the colour in a jelly Paula wants to eat.

**3** Should Paula eat the jelly? Explain your answer.

**4** What do we call this process for separating colours?

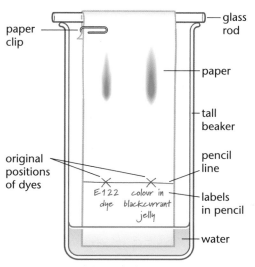

*Separating colours like this is called <u>chromatography</u>.*

## How to separate substances

To separate a mixture of substances, we need to know the **properties** of the different substances.

A factory floor is swept at the end of each day. The sweepings contains sawdust, iron filings, copper filings and salt.

**5** Look at the table of properties. Then write down how you would use apparatus in the drawings:

(a) to separate the iron filings from the sweepings;

(b) to separate the sawdust and then the sand;

(c) to separate the salt and water.

| Substance | Property |
|---|---|
| salt | dissolves in water |
| sand | does not dissolve in water |
| iron | attracted to a magnet |
| pure water | boils at 100°C |
| sawdust | floats on water |

*Use these properties as clues to separate the mixture of sweepings.*

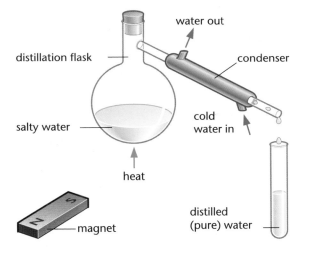

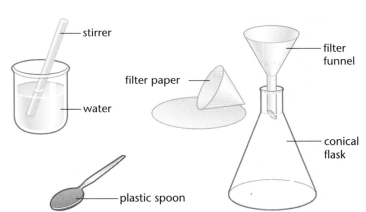

Scientists also want pure substances. They can then find out how they react to make new substances.

**6** Salt water boils at a higher temperature than pure water. How would a scientist know that the distilled water was pure?

---

### WHAT YOU NEED TO REMEMBER (Copy and complete using the **key words**)

**Separating mixtures**

Most substances in the world around us are parts of _____.

A substance that is not mixed up with other substances is called a _____ substance.

To get a pure substance, we need to _____ it from other substances.
We can do this because different substances have different _____.

# C1.9  What is density?

An important property of a material is how <u>dense</u> it is.

**REMEMBER** from pages 94 and 95

We choose materials that have the right properties for the jobs we want them to do.

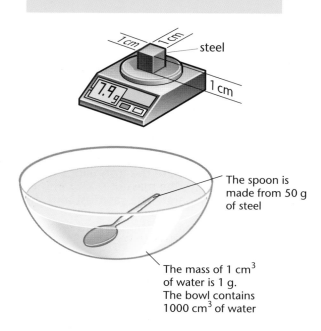

steel

The spoon is made from 50 g of steel

The mass of 1 cm³ of water is 1 g. The bowl contains 1000 cm³ of water

**1 (a)** Look at the balance in the drawing. What is the mass of 1 cm³ of steel?

**(b)** Look at the bowl of water. What mass of water is there in the bowl?

**(c)** Which has the more mass – the bowl of water or the spoon?

**(d)** Which has the more mass – 1 cm³ of water or 1 cm³ of steel?

To compare fairly how 'heavy' materials are, we should weigh the same **volume** of each one.

We can work out the density of a material like this:

$$\text{density} = \frac{\text{mass}}{\text{volume}} \text{ or mass} \div \text{volume}$$

So, for example, the density of steel is $7.9 \div 1 = 7.9 \text{ g/cm}^3$.

The density of water is $1 \text{ g/cm}^3$. We say that steel is **denser** than water.

**2 (a)** Work out the density of each of the other materials shown in the picture.

**(b)** Write down the materials in the order of their densities, starting with the lowest.

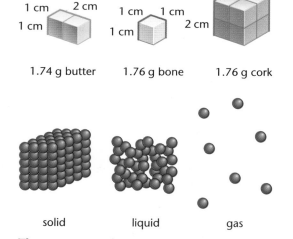

1.74 g butter      1.76 g bone      1.76 g cork

## ■ Why are gases less dense than solids and liquids?

Steam is about a thousand times less dense than ice or water. The diagrams show why.

**3** Copy and complete the sentence.

Gases are less dense than solids or liquids because their _____ are a lot further apart.

solid          liquid          gas

*The same particles make up a substance in its solid, liquid and gas states.*

## WHAT YOU NEED TO REMEMBER  (Copy and complete using the **key words**)

### What is density?

A piece of steel weighs more than the same _____ of water. So we say that steel is _____ than water.

The density of a material is its _____ divided by its volume.

CORE +
Follows on from: C1.1, C1.3

# C1.10 Density of gases

We write down the **density** of a gas in the same way as for solids and liquids.

**1 (a)** What is the normal density of air?

**(b)** How many times denser is water than air?

**2** A room is $10\,m \times 5\,m \times 3\,m$. Each cubic metre ($m^3$) is 1000 litres.

**(a)** What is the volume of the room in $m^3$?

**(b)** What is the volume of the room in litres?

**(c)** What is the mass of the air in the room?

### ■ A gas for balloons

To make a balloon rise through the air, we use a gas that is lighter than air.

**3** Which gas in the table will lift a balloon fastest through air? Give a reason for you answer.

 Find out about the airship 'Hindenberg' and explain why helium is used in modern airships.

### ■ Changing density by squeezing a gas

Unlike solids and liquids, we can **squeeze** the particles of a gas **closer** together.

**4** Look at the drawing. If we squeeze the gas so that its volume is halved, what will happen to:

**(a)** the number of particles per $cm^3$?

**(b)** the density of the gas?

**5** Can the density of a solid or a liquid be changed in this way? Explain your answer.

> **REMEMBER** from page 110
>
> Density = mass ÷ volume
>
> The density of water is $1\,g/cm^3$ or $1000\,g/litre$.

The density of air is $1.3\,g/litre$ at normal temperature and pressure.

| At normal temperature and pressure | Density (g/litre) | Other properties |
|---|---|---|
| hydrogen | 0.09 | burns easily |
| helium | 0.18 | does not burn |
| carbon dioxide | 1.98 | does not burn |
| air | 1.3 | allows other things to burn |

*The balloon rises because it is filled with a gas that is lighter than air.*

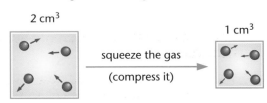

*Squeezing the particles closer together increases the number of particles per $cm^3$. This makes each cubic centimetre weigh more and so the density increases.*

**WHAT YOU NEED TO REMEMBER** (Copy and complete using the **key words**)

**Density of gases**

When you _____ a gas, the particles move _____ together.
This increases the _____ of the gas.

# C1.11  What makes a solid melt?

The diagrams show the particles in a solid and a liquid.

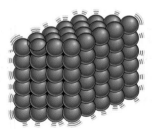

*In a solid, the forces between particles are big enough to stop them moving around. The only way they can move is to **vibrate**.*

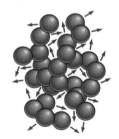

*In a liquid, the forces between particles hold them close together but do not stop them moving around.*

**1** Copy the table. Then complete it using the words 'yes' and 'no'.

|  | Solids | Liquids |
|---|---|---|
| Are there forces between the particles? |  |  |
| Do these forces stop the particles moving around? |  |  |

## ■ Heating a solid

To change a solid into a **liquid**, you need to heat it. The diagrams below show you what happens to the particles.

**2** What happens at first to the particles in a solid when you heat the solid up?

**3** What happens to the particles when the solid melts?

hot day →

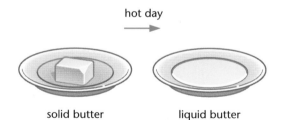

solid butter          liquid butter

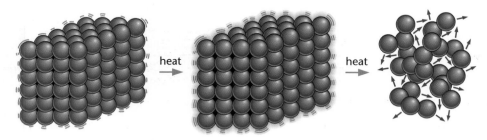

Giving energy to the particles makes them vibrate **faster**.

Eventually the vibrations become so strong that the attractive forces can't hold the particles in position any more. So the particles start to move around, but they stay in contact.

There has been a change of state from
solid ⟶ liquid.
The solid has **melted**.

**WHAT YOU NEED TO REMEMBER**  (Copy and complete using the **key words**)

**What makes a solid melt?**

When you heat up a solid, you make its particles vibrate _____.

The particles start to move around if they _____ strongly enough.
The solid has changed into a _____. It has _____.

# C1.12 Why do liquids evaporate?

When a liquid **evaporates**, it changes into a gas. There has been a change of state from liquid to gas.

The diagrams show the particles in a liquid and in a gas.

**1** Write down:

**(a)** one similarity between the particles in a liquid and in a gas;

**(b)** one difference between the particles in a liquid and in a gas.

Particles in a liquid can travel about. But forces of attraction hold them close together.

Gas particles are a long way apart. They don't affect each other except when they collide. They can move anywhere in the space available.

## How a liquid evaporates

The diagram shows how a liquid evaporates.

**2** Copy and complete the sentences.

Particles can escape from the _____ of a liquid. To do this they must be moving _____ enough.

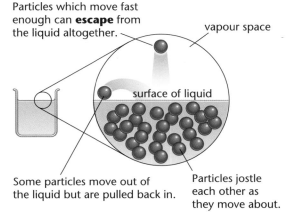

Particles which move fast enough can **escape** from the liquid altogether.

vapour space

surface of liquid

Some particles move out of the liquid but are pulled back in.

Particles jostle each other as they move about.

*In a hot liquid, more of the particles have enough **energy** to escape.*

## Evaporation and temperature

Heating a liquid makes it evaporate faster.

An evaporating liquid can also cool things down.

**3** When we get out of the sea, we often feel colder than when swimming. Explain why.

 We use a refrigerator to keep food cool.

Find out how people kept food cool before refrigerators were invented.

*To escape, water particles need energy. They get this from your body.*

**WHAT YOU NEED TO REMEMBER** (Copy and complete using the **key words**)

**Why do liquids evaporate?**

When a liquid changes into a gas, we say that it _____.

A liquid evaporates as faster moving particles _____.

Heating speeds up evaporation because more particles have enough _____ to escape.

# C1.13 Melting, boiling and temperature

When you heat up a solid, its temperature rises. The energy transferred to the particles makes them vibrate faster.

But when the solid is melting (changing to a liquid), its **temperature** stays the same. The energy transferred to the particles makes them **break away** from their fixed positions.

When all the solid has melted, the temperature starts to rise again. The energy transferred to the particles makes them move around faster.

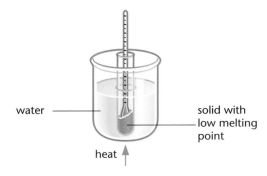

**1 (a)** Look at the graph. Then copy and complete the table.

| Part of graph | What is happening to the temperature of the substance? | What is happening to the particles of the substance? |
|---|---|---|
| A to B | | |
| B to C | | |
| C to D | | |

**(b)** What state is the substance between C and D (a solid, a liquid or a gas)?

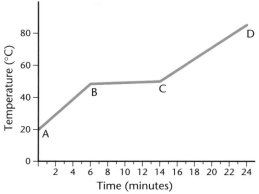

*Graph of heating up a solid.*

## ■ Boiling

When a liquid is boiling, it does not get any hotter.

**2 (a)** What happens to the energy you supply to a boiling liquid?

**(b)** What does the liquid become?

*When a liquid boils, all the energy is transferred to particles to make them **escape**.*

## WHAT YOU NEED TO REMEMBER (Copy and complete using the **key words**)

**Melting, boiling and temperature**

When a solid is melting or a liquid is boiling, its _____ doesn't change.

The energy transferred to a melting solid makes the particles _____ _____ from their fixed positions.

The energy transferred to a boiling liquid makes its particles _____ .

# C1.14  How does a gas fill its container?

The particles in a gas are a long way apart. There is hardly any force of attraction between them.

Gas particles:

- move about very fast in all directions;
- don't travel very far before they bump into each other;
- bounce off the walls of the container.

This is called rapid, **random** motion.

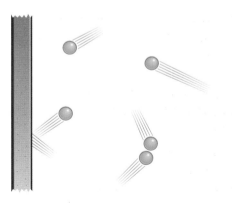

*Particles in a gas move about very fast.*

**1** Look at the diagrams.

(a) Why does the brown gas spread out through all the space in its container?

(b) Why does it take quite a long time for this to happen?

air

remove gas jar lids

brown gas

1 hour later

## ▪ Diffusion

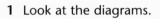

This rapid, random motion of gas molecules causes a gas to spread out as far as it can. We say that the gas **diffuses**.

We can compare how fast different gases diffuse by using a porous pot. Gas molecules can pass through the pot in both directions.

**2** Which gas diffuses fastest, hydrogen or air? Explain your answer.

**3** What would happen if the hydrogen was in the pot and the air in the beaker?

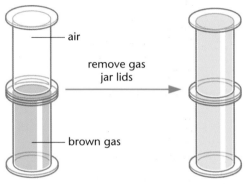

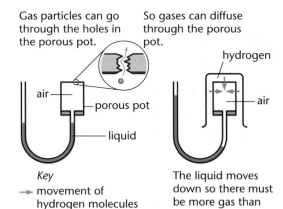

Gas particles can go through the holes in the porous pot.

So gases can diffuse through the porous pot.

hydrogen

air

porous pot

liquid

air

*Key*
→ movement of hydrogen molecules

The liquid moves down so there must be more gas than before in the pot.

**WHAT YOU NEED TO REMEMBER**  (Copy and complete using the **key words**)

**How does a gas fill its container?**

The particles of a gas move about with rapid, _____ motion.
So a gas spreads out into all the space it can. We say that the gas _____.

# C1.15  How can you change gas pressure?

You can squeeze a gas into a smaller **space**. When you do this you can feel the gas pressure pushing back.

The diagrams show why squeezing the gas changes its pressure.

1  Copy and complete the sentences.

When you squeeze a gas into a smaller space, it has a bigger _____. This is because the particles hit the _____ more often.

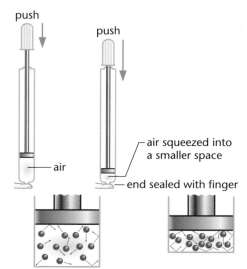

Particles hitting the piston give the gas its pressure.

The particles are squeezed closer together. They hit the piston more often. So there is a bigger pressure.

## ■ Increasing temperature, increasing pressure

Another way to increase gas pressure is to increase its **temperature**.

2  Heating a gas increases its pressure. Write down <u>two</u> reasons why.

3  What could happen if the gas pressure inside a container gets too big?

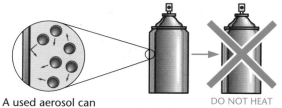

A used aerosol can still contains gas.

DO NOT HEAT

Never heat a used aerosol can up. It might burst with the pressure.

If a gas is hotter, the particles move faster. They hit the container **harder** and more **often**. So the pressure is bigger.

---

**WHAT YOU NEED TO REMEMBER**  (Copy and complete using the **key words**)

**How can you change gas pressure?**

You can increase the pressure of a gas:
- ■ by squeezing it into a smaller _____ ;

- ■ by increasing its _____, which makes its particles hit the sides of the container _____.

Both squeezing and heating the gas make its particles hit the sides of the container more _____.

# C1.16 Why do solids expand when they are heated?

A solid keeps its shape unless we make a large force act on it. This is because the particles in a solid pull each other together.

These **forces** of attraction are quite big. So they hold the particles in the same positions.

1 How can you change the shape of a solid?

2 Explain why the particles in solids cannot move around from one point to another.

*If you don't hit a nail straight, the large force will change its shape.*

## ■ What happens when we heat a solid?

The particles in a solid can't move around each other. But they still have energy so they wobble about in the same place. We say that they **vibrate**.

When we heat up a solid, we give the particles more energy.

The diagram shows what happens then.

3 An iron nail is 40 mm at room temperature. When it has been heated, it is 40.05 mm long. Explain what has happened. Use words like <u>particles</u>, <u>vibrating</u> and <u>colliding</u> in your answer.

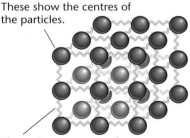

These show the centres of the particles.

The springs represent the attractive forces between them.

*In a solid, each particle attracts the particles around it. This holds the particles in position.*

*Particles in a solid can vibrate.*

when colder

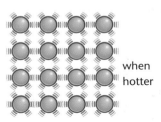

when hotter

*When particles have more energy, they make bigger vibrations. Each particle collides with its neighbours and takes up more space. So the solid **expands**.*

---

## WHAT YOU NEED TO REMEMBER (Copy and complete using the **key words**)

### Why do solids expand when they are heated?

The particles in a solid are held in position by strong _____ of attraction.
The particles can't move about but they can _____.

When a solid is heated, the vibrating particles bang into each other and take up more space, so the solid _____.

# C2.1 Two sorts of change

Gold and magnesium are both metals.
The diagrams show how these metals change when you heat them in air.

1 Copy the table and complete it using the words 'yes' and 'no'.

| | Is a new substance produced? | Is it easy to change back again? |
|---|---|---|
| Melting gold | | |
| Burning magnesium | | |

We can put all changes into two groups:

- **chemical** changes make new substances;

- **physical** changes do not make any new substances.

2 What kind of change is:

(a) melting gold?

(b) burning magnesium?

Physical changes are usually easier to change back again. We say that they are easier to **reverse**.

## ▪ Ice, water and steam

You can change ice into water and water into steam. These changes are called changes of **state**.

The diagram shows how this happens.

3 (a) Are any new substances formed during these changes?

(b) Give a reason for your answer.

4 Are the changes easy to reverse?

5 Are the changes physical or chemical?

Changes of state are physical changes.

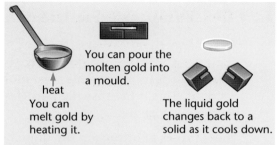

You can melt gold by heating it.

You can pour the molten gold into a mould.

The liquid gold changes back to a solid as it cools down.

*You can easily change gold from a solid to a liquid and back again as many times as you want.*

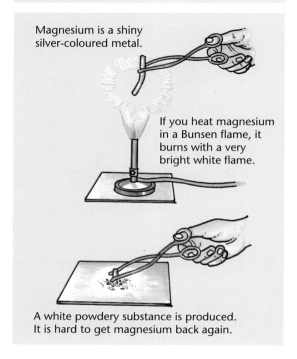

Magnesium is a shiny silver-coloured metal.

If you heat magnesium in a Bunsen flame, it burns with a very bright white flame.

A white powdery substance is produced. It is hard to get magnesium back again.

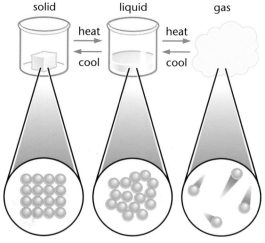

*The particles in ice, water and steam are exactly the same. So they are the <u>same</u> chemical substance in a different <u>state</u>.*

## ■ Dissolving a solid in water

The diagram shows what happens when you dissolve solid copper sulphate in water and then try to separate them again.

**6 (a)** Is dissolving a solid in water a physical or chemical change ?

**(b)** Give reasons for your answer.

Mixing things together and separating **mixtures** are physical changes.

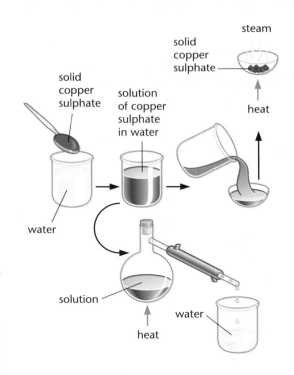

## ■ Reacting magnesium with acid

The diagrams below show what happens when magnesium reacts with dilute hydrochloric acid.

**7 (a)** What two new substances are formed in the reaction?

**(b)** Is the reaction a physical or a chemical change?

Chemical **reactions** produce chemical changes.

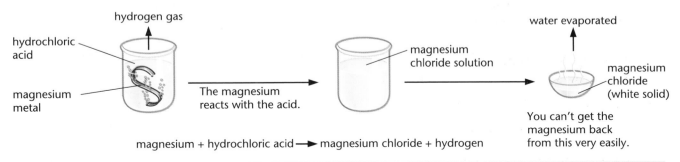

magnesium + hydrochloric acid ➔ magnesium chloride + hydrogen

---

### WHAT YOU NEED TO REMEMBER (Copy and complete using the **key words**)

**Two sorts of change**

We call changes that make new substances _____ changes.
Changes that do not make new substances are _____ changes.

Two examples of physical change are changes of _____, and separating _____.

Physical changes are usually easier to _____ than chemical changes.

Chemical changes are produced by chemical _____.

**More about physical changes: CORE+ C2.9, C2.10**

Follows on from: 1.8, 4.1, 4.8

# C2.2 Chemical reactions

When magnesium metal burns in air, changes happen. A white powdery substance is produced. It is hard to get the magnesium metal back again from this powder.

**1 (a)** Are these physical or chemical changes?

**(b)** Give a reason for your answer.

Chemical changes are produced by chemical <u>reactions</u>.

There are many different kinds of chemical reactions. Burning is just one kind. Burning is often called <u>combustion</u>.

## ■ Burning

When a match burns, a chemical reaction takes place.

**2** Look at the diagram.

**(a)** What is the wood of the match reacting with when it burns?

**(b)** What new substances are produced?

Reactions with **oxygen** are called **oxidation** reactions. So combustion, or burning, is an oxidation reaction.

But oxidation reactions do not always involve burning.

**3 (a)** Describe an oxidation reaction that doesn't involve burning.

**(b)** How can you slow down this reaction?

> **REMEMBER** from pages 118 and 119
>
> Chemical changes always make new substances.
>
> Physical changes never make new substances.

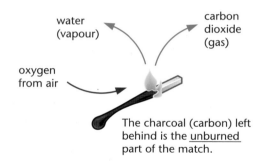

water (vapour)

carbon dioxide (gas)

oxygen from air

The charcoal (carbon) left behind is the <u>unburned</u> part of the match.

*Fats like butter or margarine go 'off' if you keep them too long. This is because they react with the oxygen from the air. This reaction is slower when the fat is cold. That's why it's best to keep it in the fridge.*

## Splitting up chemicals by heating them

If you heat some substances, they split into different substances. The diagrams show what happens when you heat copper carbonate.

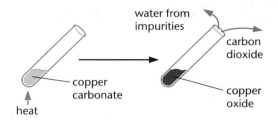

4 What substances does copper carbonate split up into when it is heated?

5 How can you tell that the gas given off is carbon dioxide?

Splitting up a substance by **heating** it is called <u>thermal decomposition</u>.

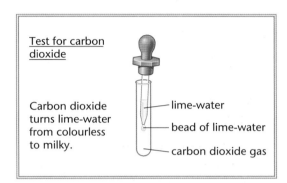

Test for carbon dioxide

Carbon dioxide turns lime-water from colourless to milky.

lime-water
bead of lime-water
carbon dioxide gas

## Splitting up chemicals using electricity

You can split up some substances by passing an **electric current** through them. You have to dissolve the substance in water or melt it first. The diagram shows what happens when you pass an electric current through copper chloride solution.

6 What two substances are produced when you pass electricity through the copper chloride solution?

7 How can you show that the gas produced is chlorine?

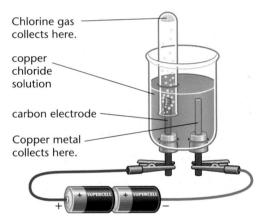

Chlorine gas collects here.

copper chloride solution

carbon electrode

Copper metal collects here.

(Note: most of the chlorine gas that is produced in the reaction shown dissolves in the copper chloride solution.)

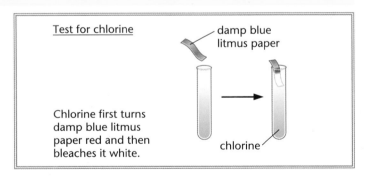

Test for chlorine

damp blue litmus paper

Chlorine first turns damp blue litmus paper red and then bleaches it white.

chlorine

## WHAT YOU NEED TO REMEMBER (Copy and complete using the **key words**)

### Chemical reactions

Another name for burning is combustion. When things burn they react with _____.
So we also call burning an _____ reaction.

In a thermal decomposition reaction, you split up a substance by _____ it.

In electrolysis, you split up a substance by passing an _____ _____ through it.

121

Follows on from: 2.5, 2.6

# C2.3  Elements and atoms

There are millions of different substances. But they are made from about 90 simple substances joined together in different ways.

These simple substances are called **elements**.

### ■ How do we know which substances are elements?

**1** Write down two things you can do to try to split up a substance.

If you <u>can</u> split a substance up, it <u>isn't</u> an element.

If you <u>can't</u> split a substance up, it <u>is</u> probably an element.

**2** Look at the diagrams on this page. Then copy and complete the table using the words 'yes' and 'no'.

| Substance | Can you split it up? | Is it an element? |
|---|---|---|
| copper chloride | | |
| copper | | |
| chlorine | | |
| mercury oxide | | |
| mercury | | |
| oxygen | | |

**3** How do you know that heating mercury oxide produces oxygen gas?

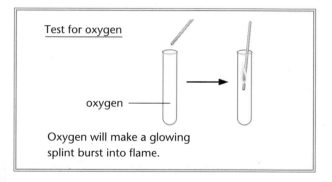

Test for oxygen

oxygen

Oxygen will make a glowing splint burst into flame.

REMEMBER from page 121

There are two main ways of splitting up a substance:
- heating it;
- dissolving it in water or melting it, and then passing an electric current through it.

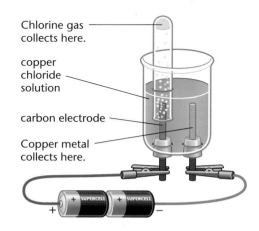

Chlorine gas collects here.

copper chloride solution

carbon electrode

Copper metal collects here.

*You can split up copper chloride. But you can't split copper or chlorine into anything simpler.*

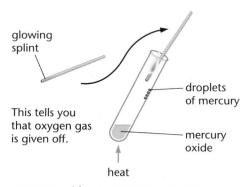

glowing splint

This tells you that oxygen gas is given off.

droplets of mercury

mercury oxide

heat

mercury oxide → mercury + oxygen

*You can split up mercury oxide. But you can't split mercury or oxygen into anything simpler. (Note: Mercury is very poisonous. This experiment must be done only by the teacher using a fume cupboard.)*

## Getting copper from copper carbonate

The diagram shows how you can get copper metal starting from copper carbonate.

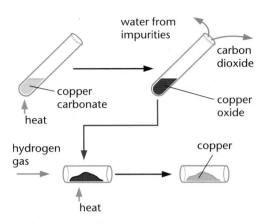

water from impurities

carbon dioxide

copper carbonate

copper oxide

heat

hydrogen gas

copper

heat

**4** Copy and complete the sentences.

We heat copper carbonate to get copper _____.

Then we heat copper oxide with _____ gas. The copper oxide changes to _____.

In this reaction, hydrogen takes the oxygen out of the copper _____ and joins with oxygen to form water.

## What are elements made of?

An element is made of tiny particles called **atoms**.

An element is a simple substance. This is because it is made up of the **same** kind of atom.

**5** Look at the top diagram. Write down the chemicals that you know are not elements.

**6** How is an argon atom different from a helium atom?

Helium is an element. Helium atoms are all the same size as each other.

Argon is an element. Argon atoms are bigger and heavier than helium atoms.

*Atoms of different elements are **different** from each other.*

## The element chart

Scientists put the elements into a special chart called the periodic table.

**7** Are there more metals or more non-metals amongst the elements?

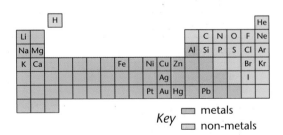

*Key*  □ metals
□ non-metals

---

**WHAT YOU NEED TO REMEMBER** (Copy and complete using the **key words**)

**Elements and atoms**

We call simple substances _____.

Elements are made up of very small particles called _____.

All the atoms in one element are the _____ kind.

Atoms of different elements are _____.

**More about elements: CORE+ C2.11**

# C2.4 Compounds

We know that there are only about 90 elements that are found in nature. But elements can join together. They make millions of different substances called **compounds**.

**1** How many different pairs of letters can you make from A, B and C?

AB AC ...

The more letters we have, then the more pairs we can get.

**2** How many different pairs of letters can you make from A, B, C and D?

AB AC ... ... ... CD

When elements join together to make compounds, their different atoms 'stick' to each other. We say that atoms join together by making chemical <u>bonds</u>.

**3** Look at the diagrams. Then copy and complete the table.

| Name of substance | What atoms is it made of? | Element or compound? |
|---|---|---|
| copper | | |
| copper oxide | | |
| water | | |
| hydrogen | | |
| oxygen | | |

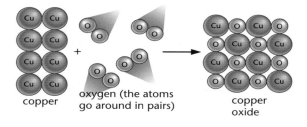

copper + oxygen (the atoms go around in pairs) → copper oxide

## ■ Differences between compounds and mixtures

A **mixture** of hydrogen and oxygen is very dangerous. The diagram shows why.

**4** Copy and complete the sentences.

A flame will make a mixture of hydrogen and oxygen _____. The atoms of hydrogen and oxygen _____ together. This makes a _____ called water.

In a mixture, the particles of oxygen and hydrogen are mixed but not joined.

A spark or flame makes the mixture explode.

The oxygen and hydrogen atoms join together to make a compound called water.

## Compounds and their elements are different

The **properties** of a compound are very different from the properties of its elements.

For example, hydrogen and oxygen are both gases. The compound they produce when they react is the liquid we call water.

Look at the picture.

Mercury oxide

5 Copy and complete the sentences using these words:
mercury, solid, oxygen, liquid, gas.

Mercury oxide is a red _____. It is made from the elements _____ and _____.

Mercury is a silver-coloured _____. Oxygen is a colourless _____.

methane

water

## Names of compounds

You can often tell what elements are in a compound from its name.

The name <u>mercury oxide</u>, for example, tells us that it is a compound of the elements <u>mercury</u> and <u>oxygen</u>.

The names of some compounds don't tell you what elements they contain. You just have to remember.

ammonia

6 Copy and complete the table by writing down the elements in each of the compounds.

| Compound | Elements in the compound |
|---|---|
| mercury oxide | mercury and oxygen |
| water | |
| magnesium oxide | |
| methane | |
| ammonia | |
| copper chloride | |

**WHAT YOU NEED TO REMEMBER** (Copy and complete using the **key words**)

**Compounds**

Substances made from atoms of different elements joined together are called _____.

A substance made from different atoms <u>not</u> joined together is called a _____.

Compounds have different _____ from the elements they are made from.

**More about compounds: CORE+ C2.11 to C2.15**

# C2.5   Elements reacting with oxygen

REMEMBER from page 50

Compounds called <u>oxides</u> contain oxygen joined to a different element.

Many elements will burn in oxygen to make oxides. The atoms of the element join up with atoms of oxygen.

We call these reactions **oxidation** reactions.

1  (a)  What is the everyday name for hydrogen oxide?

   (b)  Write down the name of <u>two</u> other oxides.

*Hydrogen oxide*

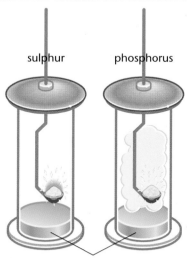

sulphur          phosphorus

litmus solution after the reactions

## ■ Burning non-metallic elements

Many non-metallic elements burn in oxygen to make **oxides**.

The diagrams show what these oxides do to litmus solution.

2  Copy and complete the sentences.

   Some non-metal oxides make litmus solution go _____. This tells you that these non-metal oxides are _____.

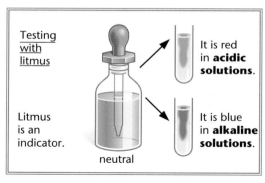

Testing with litmus

Litmus is an indicator.

neutral

It is red in **acidic solutions**.

It is blue in **alkaline solutions**.

## ■ Burning metallic elements

Metallic elements also burn in oxygen to make <u>oxides</u>.

Some metal oxides dissolve in water. The diagrams show what these metal oxides do to litmus solution.

3  Copy and complete the sentences.

   Metal oxides that dissolve in water make the litmus go _____. This tells you that these metal oxides are _____.

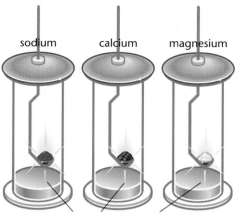

sodium      calcium      magnesium

litmus solution after the reaction

sodium + oxygen → sodium oxide
calcium + oxygen → calcium oxide
magnesium + oxygen → magnesium oxide

## How oxygen got its name

More than 200 years ago, a Frenchman called Lavoisier was doing experiments with a 'new kind of air'.

He found that non-metals burned brightly in this gas to make acids. So he called the gas 'oxygen'. It means 'acid maker'. The elements sodium, calcium and magnesium were not discovered until after Lavoisier died.

4 Explain why Lavoisier called the 'new kind of air' oxygen.

5 Why is the name not really very suitable?

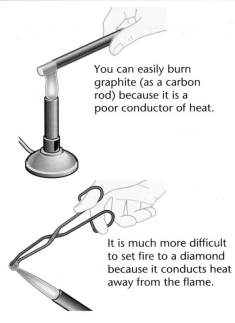

You can easily burn graphite (as a carbon rod) because it is a poor conductor of heat.

It is much more difficult to set fire to a diamond because it conducts heat away from the flame.

## Carbon – metal or non-metal?

Diamond and graphite are very different forms of the element carbon. They have some of the properties of non-metals. But they also have some properties of metals.

6 Look at the pictures and then copy and complete the table.

| Form of carbon | Conducts heat? | Conducts electricity? | Is the oxide acidic? |
|---|---|---|---|
| diamond | yes | | |
| graphite (carbon rod) | no | | |

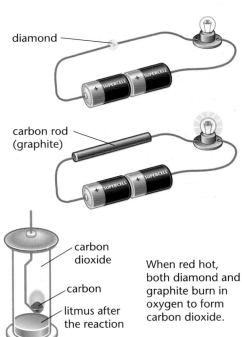

diamond

carbon rod (graphite)

carbon dioxide

carbon

litmus after the reaction

When red hot, both diamond and graphite burn in oxygen to form carbon dioxide.

7 Copy and complete the sentences.

Both forms of carbon burn in oxygen to make an oxide that turns litmus red. So carbon must be a _____.

**WHAT YOU NEED TO REMEMBER** (Copy and complete using the **key words**)

**Elements reacting with oxygen**

When we burn elements in oxygen, we get compounds called _____.

We say that these are _____ reactions.

Some non-metallic elements make oxides that dissolve in water to make _____.

Some metals make oxides that dissolve in water to make _____.

**More about reactions: CORE+ C2.16**

Follows on from:
3.8, 4.6, 4.7, 4.9

# C2.6 Metals reacting with acids

Most metals will burn in oxygen to make oxides.

Many metals will also react with dilute **acids**.

## ■ How fast do they react?

Some pupils studied the reaction between dilute hydrochloric acid and the metals zinc, iron and magnesium. The balloons are to catch any gas that is made in the reactions.

1 How did the pupils make sure that their experiment was fair?

2 At the end of the experiment:

(a) which balloon was biggest?

(b) which metal reacted fastest?

(c) which balloon did not get much bigger?

(d) which metal reacted slowest?

The metal that reacts fastest is the <u>most reactive</u> metal.

3 Write down the three metals in order of their reactivity, putting the most reactive first and the least reactive last.

A list of metals in order of their reactivity is called a <u>reactivity series</u>.

## ■ Adding more metals to the reactivity series

The diagrams tell you about the reactions of gold and copper.

4 Add gold and copper to your reactivity series.

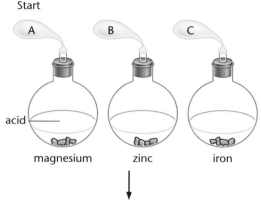

Start

There is the same amount of acid and the same amount of metal in each flask.

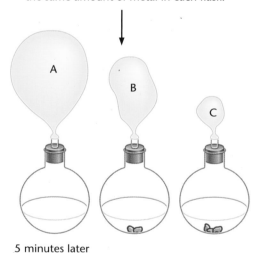

5 minutes later

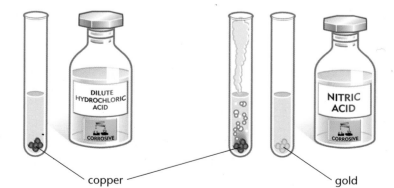

Copper does not react with dilute hydrochloric acid.

Concentrated nitric acid will react with copper, but not with gold.

## What new substances are produced?

The diagrams tell you about the substances produced when zinc reacts with dilute hydrochloric acid.

**5** What <u>two</u> substances are produced in the reaction?

**6** How do we know that the gas produced is hydrogen?

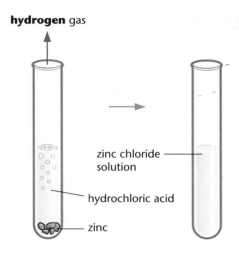

**hydrogen** gas

zinc chloride solution

hydrochloric acid

zinc

## Word equations

Here is a convenient way of writing down what happens in the reaction between zinc and dilute hydrochloric acid.

**zinc** + hydrochloric acid → zinc **chloride** + hydrogen

This is called a <u>word equation</u>.

The metal compounds produced in reactions like this are called **salts**. So we can write:

metal + acid → a salt + hydrogen

**7 (a)** What salt would be produced in the reaction between magnesium and hydrochloric acid?

**(b)** Write a word equation for this reaction.

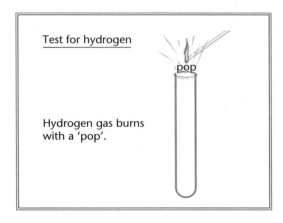

Test for hydrogen

pop

Hydrogen gas burns with a 'pop'.

---

**WHAT YOU NEED TO REMEMBER** (Copy and complete using the **key words**)

**Metals reacting with acids**

Most metals react with dilute _____. The reactions produce a gas called _____. They also produce compounds called _____.

We can write down the reaction between zinc and hydrochloric acid like this:

_____ + dilute hydrochloric acid → zinc _____ + hydrogen

**More about reactivity series: CORE+ C2.17**

Follows on from: 3.7, 3.8, 4.9

# C2.7  Displacement reactions

A more **reactive** metal will push a less reactive metal out of a **solution** of one of its compounds. We say that the more reactive metal <u>displaces</u> the less reactive one. We call this sort of reaction a **displacement** reaction.

The diagram shows you an example of this.

1 Copy and complete the following.

zinc + copper nitrate → zinc nitrate + _____
(metal)   (solution)      (solution)      (metal)

This reaction shows that zinc is a more _____ metal than copper.

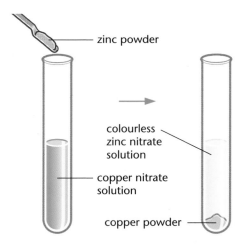

zinc powder

colourless zinc nitrate solution

copper nitrate solution

copper powder

### ■ Looking at displacement reactions

A group of pupils does an experiment.

To each 1 cm square piece of zinc, they add 2 drops of a solution of a different metal compound.

They watch for small crystals of the metal from the solution growing on the surface of the zinc square.

The illustration shows crystals of lead. These grow on the surface of the zinc. This happens because zinc is more reactive than lead. Zinc particles go into the solution and push out the lead particles.

Look at the results. Where crystals have grown, the drawings are shaded.

2 Copy and complete the results table for this experiment.

3 (a) Write down a list of metals that are less reactive than zinc.

 (b) Which metal may be more reactive than zinc?

 (c) How could you find out for sure?

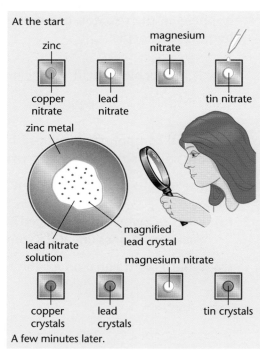

At the start

zinc

copper nitrate

lead nitrate

magnesium nitrate

tin nitrate

zinc metal

lead nitrate solution

magnified lead crystal

magnesium nitrate

copper crystals

lead crystals

tin crystals

A few minutes later.

| Solution of metal nitrate | Did crystals form on zinc? |
|---|---|
| copper | |
| lead | ✓ |
| magnesium | |
| tin | |

## More displacement reactions

The pupils test 1 cm square pieces of tin in the same way.

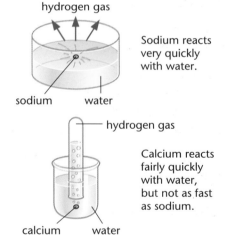

tin

copper nitrate | lead nitrate | magnesium nitrate | zinc nitrate

copper crystals | lead crystals

**4 (a)** Which <u>two</u> metals does tin displace?

**(b)** Which <u>two</u> metals are less reactive than tin?

The pupils test other metal squares – copper, lead and magnesium. They put these results, and the results from the first two experiments, into a table.

| Solution of metal nitrate | Metals | | | | |
|---|---|---|---|---|---|
| | zinc | tin | magnesium | lead | copper |
| copper | ✓ | ✓ | ✓ | ✓ | |
| lead | ✓ | ✓ | ✓ | | ✗ |
| magnesium | ✗ | ✗ | | ✗ | ✗ |
| tin | ✓ | | ✓ | ✗ | ✗ |
| zinc | | ✗ | ✓ | ✗ | ✗ |

*Key:* ✓ *indicates that crystals formed on the metal.*

## Looking at results

The most reactive of these metals is the one that displaces the most metals (gets the most ticks).

**5** Write out these metals in the order of their reactivities, starting with the most reactive and going down to the least reactive.

A list of metals in the order of their reactivities is called a **reactivity series**.

## Two very reactive metals

Sodium and calcium are very reactive metals. But you can't use them to displace other metals from solutions.

**6** Explain why.

**7** Add sodium and calcium to your reactivity series.

hydrogen gas

Sodium reacts very quickly with water.

sodium    water

hydrogen gas

Calcium reacts fairly quickly with water, but not as fast as sodium.

calcium    water

---

### WHAT YOU NEED TO REMEMBER (Copy and complete using the **key words**)

**Displacement reactions**

Some metals are more _____ than others.

A reactive metal will push a less reactive metal out of a _____ of one of its compounds. We call this type of chemical change a _____ reaction.

A list of metals in order of their reactivities is called a _____ _____.

**More about displacement: CORE+ C2.18**

# C2.8 Carrying out tests

## Three common gases

Oxygen, hydrogen and carbon dioxide are all gases. All of them are colourless and all of them have no smell. So if we get a colourless gas in a chemical reaction we need to <u>test</u> it to find out what it is.

The diagrams show the **chemical tests** for these gases, but they don't tell you which is which.

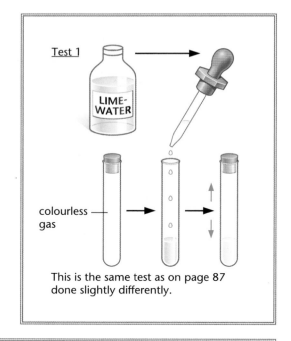

Test 1

This is the same test as on page 87 done slightly differently.

1 Copy and complete the sentences.

We use lime-water to test for

_____ _____.

This gas makes the lime-water go

_____.

(See page 87 if you are not sure.)

We use a lighted splint to test for

_____.

This gas burns with a slight _____.
(See page 129 if you are not sure.)

We use a glowing splint to test for

_____.

This gas makes the glowing splint

_____.

(See page 122 if you are not sure.)

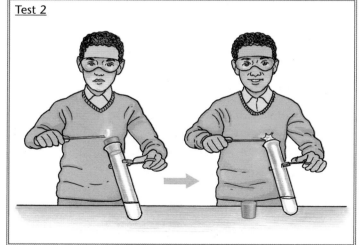

Test 2

Test 3

## Using litmus

Litmus is a very useful dye. It can tell us whether a solution is an acid or an alkali or neutral (like water). We say that litmus is an <u>indicator</u>.
We can also use litmus to test for a gas called chlorine.

2  Look at the diagrams. Then copy and complete the table.

| Colour of litmus | What this tells you |
|---|---|
| red | |
| purple | |
| blue | |
| white | |

Hydrogen and oxygen are neutral gases but carbon dioxide will turn litmus, or moist litmus paper, red.

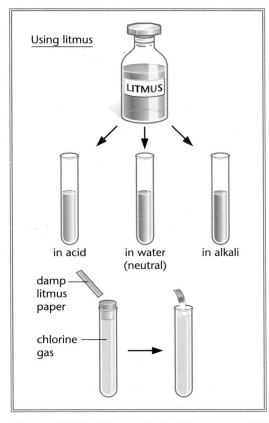

Using litmus

in acid    in water (neutral)    in alkali

damp litmus paper

chlorine gas

## Testing for water

Many colourless liquids are neutral. So just because a liquid turns litmus purple, it does <u>not</u> mean that the liquid is water.

We can also test liquids with blue cobalt chloride paper.

3  (a)  What colour does the paper turn in water?

   (b)  What can you say about liquid X?

Many solutions contain water and would change the colour of the cobalt chloride.

4  How could you prove whether liquid Y is <u>pure</u> water?

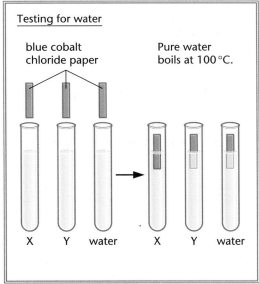

Testing for water

blue cobalt chloride paper

Pure water boils at 100 °C.

X    Y    water    X    Y    water

---

**WHAT YOU NEED TO REMEMBER**  (Copy and complete using the **key words**)

**Carrying out tests**

When we want to find out what a substance is, we carry out chemical _____.
Most tests are _____ changes.

*You need to know what each of these tests tells you.*

# C2.9  Physical change and mass

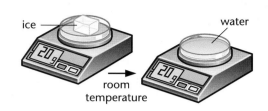

ice → water
room temperature

Melting ice is a physical change. Dissolving sugar in water is also a physical change. This is because no new substances are made.

**1** What happens to the total mass:

  **(a)** when ice melts?

  **(b)** when sugar dissolves in water?

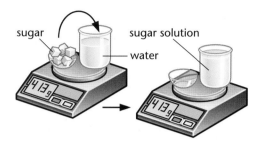

sugar • water → sugar solution

## ■ Why does the mass stay the same?

Water and sugar, like everything else, are made of particles.

When we melt ice or dissolve sugar in water, we still have exactly the same number of particles.

**2** Leo is making a cup of soup. He adds 100 g of soup powder to 500 g of hot water and stirs until all the powder dissolves.

  **(a)** What is the mass of his soup?

  **(b)** Explain your answer. Use the words 'particles' and 'mass' in your answer.

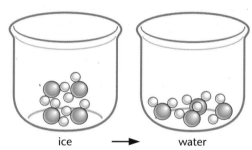

ice → water

The molecules are not shown to scale.

*If we still have exactly the same **particles**, then we have exactly the same **mass**.*

## ■ Why does mass sometimes seem to change?

If you leave a beaker of water for a few days, the mass of the water does seem to change.

Water molecules escape from the beaker into the air. You would have to weigh the whole Earth to show that there was no change in mass!

**3 (a)** Explain how puddles 'dry up' once it's stopped raining.

  **(b)** What happens to the mass of the puddle? Explain your answer.

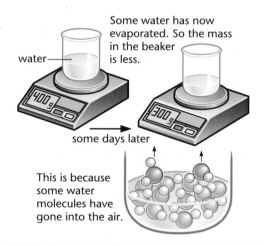

water

Some water has now evaporated. So the mass in the beaker is less.

some days later

This is because some water molecules have gone into the air.

---

**WHAT YOU NEED TO REMEMBER** (Copy and complete using the **key words**)

**Physical change and mass**

In a physical change you still have the same substances made from the same _____.
So in a physical change there is no change in _____.

# C2.10 Chemical change and mass

Hydrogen reacts with oxygen to make water. But there are still the same atoms, so there is no change in mass.

In chemical reactions, atoms of different elements combine in **different** ways to make new substances.

But all the **atoms** must still be there. So the **mass** of the new substances (the <u>products</u>) must be exactly the same as the mass of the substances you started with (the <u>reactants</u>).

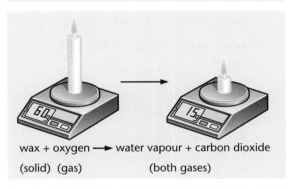

wax + oxygen ⟶ water vapour + carbon dioxide
(solid) (gas)                (both gases)

### ■ Explaining apparent changes in mass

In many chemical reactions, the mass does seem to change. We need to be able to explain why.

1 What seems to happen to the mass:

 (a) when a candle burns?

 (b) when magnesium burns?

2 Explain each of these changes of mass.

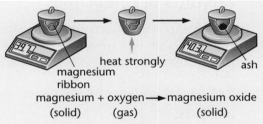

magnesium + oxygen ⟶ magnesium oxide
(solid)        (gas)         (solid)

You lift the lid of the crucible a little way every minute or so to let air in so that the magnesium can burn. You put the lid back down to trap as much of the magnesium oxide ash as possible. This is what you need to weigh.

### ■ Testing your explanations

To check that mass doesn't change when something burns, you need to burn it inside a sealed container.

The experiment shown in the diagram was done by the famous chemist called Lavoisier more than 200 years ago.

3 (a) Write a word equation for the reaction shown in the diagram.

 (b) Explain why there is no change in mass.

4 Look again at the magnesium reaction. What mass of oxygen combined with the magnesium?

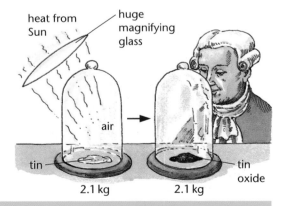

## WHAT YOU NEED TO REMEMBER  (Copy and complete using the **key words**)

### Chemical change and mass

In chemical reactions, there is no change in _____.
This is because there are still the same _____.
They are just joined together in _____ ways.

# C2.11  Different kinds of mixtures

We know that elements can react and combine to make new substances. We call these substances chemical compounds. But if we put two or more elements together and they do not react, then what we have is a **mixture** of elements.

Look at the picture of the diver and also at the table below.

**1** Write down the name of <u>one</u> mixture made up of <u>elements</u> that are:

**(a)** solids   **(b)** gases.

Breathing gas
helium
oxygen

Bubbles
helium
oxygen
carbon dioxide
water vapour

Stainless steel
iron
carbon
nickel

Sea-water
water
salts

## ◼ Mixtures of compounds

Pure compounds just contain the single compound. But just as we can have a mixture of elements, so we can have a mixture of different **compounds**.

**2** Write down <u>one</u> mixture of different <u>compounds</u> given in the picture.

**3** Explain why we do <u>not</u> say sea-water is a pure compound.

## ◼ Mixtures of elements and compounds

We can also **mix** different kinds of substances together, such as elements and compounds.

**4** Write down <u>one</u> mixture in the photograph which contains both elements and compounds.

**5** Copy and complete the table on the right.

| Name of mixture | Ingredient of mixture | Element or compound? |
|---|---|---|
| stainless steel | iron | element |
| | carbon | _____ |
| | _____ | _____ |
| breathing gas | helium | _____ |
| | _____ | element |
| bubbles | helium | element |
| | oxygen | _____ |
| | carbon dioxide | _____ |
| | water vapour | compound |
| _____ | water | compound |
| | salts | compound |

**WHAT YOU NEED TO REMEMBER** (Copy and complete using the **key words**)

**Different kinds of mixtures**

We can have a _____ of elements, or of _____.
We can also _____ elements and compounds together.

# C2.12 More about compounds and mixtures

We can <u>mix</u> hydrogen and oxygen gases together in any amounts. This makes mixtures of the same substances but in different **ratios**.

The drawings show two mixtures of hydrogen and oxygen gas being made.

**1 (a)** Copy and complete the table.

| Mixture | Number of hydrogen molecules for each oxygen molecule | Ratio of hydrogen molecules to oxygen molecules |
|---------|------------------------|------------------------|
| A | | |
| B | | |

**(b)** Mixture C contains 5 million hydrogen molecules and 1 million oxygen molecules. Add an extra row to your table to show this information.

So a mixture of hydrogen and oxygen can be in <u>any</u> proportions.

## ■ Hydrogen and oxygen reacting

The diagram shows what happens when hydrogen and oxygen react.

**2** Copy and complete the sentences.

Hydrogen burns in oxygen to form a compound called _____. In each molecule of water there is 1 atom of _____ and 2 atoms of _____.
So, in water, the ratio of hydrogen atoms to oxygen atoms is always _____.

In water, as in all other compounds, the ratio of atoms is always the **same**. We say that compounds have a fixed **composition**.

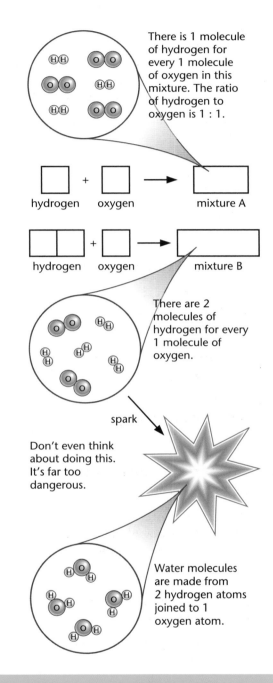

There is 1 molecule of hydrogen for every 1 molecule of oxygen in this mixture. The ratio of hydrogen to oxygen is 1 : 1.

hydrogen + oxygen → mixture A

hydrogen + oxygen → mixture B

There are 2 molecules of hydrogen for every 1 molecule of oxygen.

spark

Don't even think about doing this. It's far too dangerous.

Water molecules are made from 2 hydrogen atoms joined to 1 oxygen atom.

**WHAT YOU NEED TO REMEMBER** (Copy and complete using the **key words**)

### More about compounds and mixtures

In a mixture, elements can be mixed together in different _____.

But in a compound, the atoms of the different elements are always joined together in the _____ ratio. We say that compounds have a fixed _____.

# C2.13  Simple chemical formulas

**REMEMBER** from page 137

In a chemical compound, the atoms of different elements are always in the same ratio.

Every element has a chemical symbol. This is a quick way of writing down an element.

1  Write down these elements in a list: carbon, chlorine, copper, hydrogen, oxygen, sodium, sulphur and zinc. Alongside each name write down the symbol for that element.
[An old name for sodium is 'natrium'.]

**The symbols for some elements**

| H | C | Cl | Cu |
|---|---|----|----|
| Na | O | S | Zn |

We can use chemical symbols to show the atoms in a compound.

The diagrams show the atoms in sodium chloride and in water.

2  Copy and complete the table.

| Compound | Ratio of atoms in the compound | Formula |
|----------|-------------------------------|---------|
| sodium chloride | 1 sodium atom for every 1 _____ atom | |
| water | 2 _____ atoms for every 1 oxygen atom | |
| carbon dioxide | 2 oxygen atoms for every 1 _____ atom | |
| | 1 copper atom for every 1 oxygen atom | |

The box tells you the formulas of some more compounds.

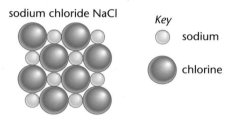

sodium chloride NaCl

Key
○ sodium
● chlorine

Sodium and chlorine atoms are in the ratio 1 : 1. So the formula for sodium chloride is NaCl.

Cl — Na — Cl — Na
  |      |      |      |
Na — Cl — Na — Cl
  |      |      |      |
Cl — Na — Cl — Na
  |      |      |      |
Na — Cl — Na — Cl

Key
○ hydrogen
● oxygen

water

Hydrogen and oxygen atoms are in the ratio 2 : 1. So the formula for water is $H_2O$.

3  (a)  Copy and complete the sentence.

   In hydrogen chloride there is 1 atom of hydrogen for every 1 atom of _____.

   (b)  Write a similar sentence about each of the other compounds in the box.

**The formulas of some compounds**

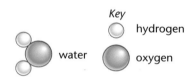

| hydrogen chloride | HCl |
| copper sulphide | CuS |
| copper chloride | $CuCl_2$ |
| sodium oxide | $Na_2O$ |

## WHAT YOU NEED TO REMEMBER

**Simple chemical formulas**

*You should be able to use the formula of a compound to tell you what elements are in the compound and the ratio of their atoms.*

# C2.14  More about chemical formulas

You have already learned how to write down the chemical formulas of chemical compounds.

**1** Write down the chemical formula for:

    **(a)** methane,

    **(b)** magnesium oxide.

methane        magnesium oxide

## ■ Formulas of elements

Atoms of oxygen and some other elements that are gases go about in <u>pairs</u>.
These pairs of atoms are called **molecules**.
Each of these molecules also has a formula.

oxygen molecule     nitrogen molecule
formula $O_2$

**2** Draw a nitrogen molecule.
Underneath, write its formula.

**3** Some of the gases in air are elements and others are compounds.

Draw a table with these headings, then put the formula for each gas in the correct column.

| Elements | Compounds |
|---|---|
|  |  |

**4** Some of the gases in air are single atoms, others are molecules.

Draw a table with these headings, then put the formula for each gas in the correct column.

| Single atoms | Molecules |
|---|---|
|  |  |

*Air is a mixture of gases.*
*These are the chemical formulas for some of the gases in the air.*

Ar         $CO_2$         Ne

$N_2$         $O_2$

$SO_2$         $H_2O$

The formula for a gas that goes around as single atoms is just its symbol.

**WHAT YOU NEED TO REMEMBER**  (Copy and complete using the **key words**)

**More about chemical formulas**

The atoms of some elements go around in pairs called _____.

139

# C2.15  More complicated chemical formulas

Most of the compounds we have seen so far have been compounds of two elements only.

Some compounds we have met before involve three elements.

**1** Read the box about formula rules. Then write down how many atoms of each of these elements there are in one molecule of glucose.

**(a)** carbon **(b)** hydrogen **(c)** oxygen

**2** Now do the same for the elements in the formulas of:

**(a)** nitric acid $HNO_3$

**(b)** sulphuric acid $H_2SO_4$

| Element | Symbol |
|---|---|
| hydrogen | H |
| carbon | C |
| chlorine | Cl |
| copper | Cu |
| sodium | Na |
| oxygen | O |
| sulphur | S |
| zinc | Zn |

**Formula rules**

<u>Rule 1:</u> The symbol of the element by itself means one atom of the element. For example, in hydrochloric acid (HCl), there is one hydrogen atom.

<u>Rule 2:</u> If there is a number after the symbol, this says how many atoms there are of the element. For example, in glucose:

$$C_6H_{12}O_6$$

This tells us there are 6 atoms of carbon.   12 atoms of hydrogen   How many atoms of oxygen?

<u>Rule 3:</u> If there are brackets, the number just after the brackets multiplies everything inside.

$$Zn(NO_3)_2$$

This multiplies everything inside by 2.

## ■ The 'ate' compounds

Compounds containing a metal always start with the name of the metal. If they also contain oxygen and another non-metal, the name often ends in 'ate'.

Look at the names and formulas of some 'ate' compounds.

**3** For each of the 'ate' compounds shown, write down how many atoms there are for each element in the formula.

**4** Write down the names of the elements in the following compounds:

potassium nitrate, copper carbonate, zinc sulphate

**5** Explain how the name of an 'ate' compound depends upon the name of the other non-metal.

**Some 'ate' compounds**

| | |
|---|---|
| zinc carbonate | $ZnCO_3$ |
| copper sulphate | $CuSO_4$ |
| zinc nitrate | $Zn(NO_3)_2$ |

## WHAT YOU NEED TO REMEMBER

**More complicated chemical formulas**

*You need to be able to work out which elements are in a compound (and what numbers of atoms they have) just as you have for the compounds on this page.*

# C2.16  Energy changes in chemical reactions

## ■ Reactions that give out energy

When things burn, **energy** is given out.

The diagram shows what happens when hydrogen burns.

1  Copy and complete the sentence.

When hydrogen burns, _____ atoms join up with _____ atoms to make _____ of water.

When atoms of two elements join together, the reaction usually gives out energy.

The forces that join atoms together are called <u>bonds</u>.

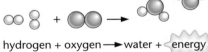

hydrogen + oxygen ⟶ water + energy

Bonds between hydrogen atoms and bonds between oxygen atoms are broken.

New bonds between hydrogen and oxygen atoms are formed.

## ■ Reactions that take in energy

To **split** a compound into simpler substances, we usually have to put energy in.

2  What can you do to zinc carbonate to split it into simpler substances?

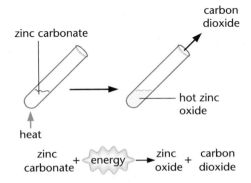

zinc carbonate + energy ⟶ zinc oxide + carbon dioxide

## ■ Now try these

The diagrams show two more reactions.

3  (a)  Copy the word equation for each reaction.

(b)  Add energy to the correct side of each equation.

(c)  Which bonds are broken and which bonds are formed in each reaction?

hydrogen + chlorine ⟶ hydrogen chloride
(Hydrogen burns in chlorine.)

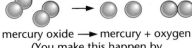

mercury oxide ⟶ mercury + oxygen
(You make this happen by heating mercury oxide.)

---

**WHAT YOU NEED TO REMEMBER**  (Copy and complete using the **key words**)

**Energy changes in chemical reactions**

When the atoms of two elements join together, the reaction usually gives out _____.

Reactions which _____ up compounds take energy in.

# C2.17 More about the reactivity series

| Reactivity series for metals | | |
|---|---|---|
| sodium | | most reactive |
| calcium | | |
| magnesium | | |
| aluminium | | |
| zinc | | |
| iron | | |
| lead | | |
| copper | | least reactive |

As we go from the top to the bottom of the reactivity series, the metals become less reactive.

1  For each of the following pairs of metals, write down which one is the more reactive.

  (a)  calcium or sodium

  (b)  magnesium or zinc

  (c)  iron or copper

  (d)  lead or calcium

## ■ Reaction with water

| sodium | very fast reaction with cold water |
|---|---|
| calcium | fast reaction with cold water |
| magnesium | burns when heated in steam |
| aluminium | no reaction |
| zinc | reacts when heated in steam |
| iron | reacts when heated to red heat in steam |
| lead | dissolves very slowly over many years |
| copper | no reaction |

2  (a)  Which metal does not react as you would expect?

  (b)  This metal is used to make window frames. Explain why it can be used like this.

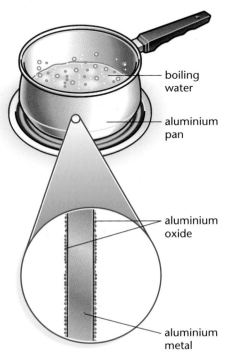

boiling water

aluminium pan

aluminium oxide

aluminium metal

aluminium oxide

*Aluminium is a reactive metal. So it quickly gets covered with a thin layer of aluminium oxide. This layer is very tough. It protects the aluminium underneath.*

## ■ What happens when metals react with water?

The word equation shows the products that are made when sodium reacts with water.

sodium + water → **hydrogen** + sodium **hydroxide**

3  (a)  Which product burns with a 'pop' when you light it?

  (b)  Which product turns litmus blue?

  (c)  Write a word equation for the reaction of calcium with water.

---

**WHAT YOU NEED TO REMEMBER**  (Copy and complete using the **key words**)

**More about the reactivity series**

When a metal reacts with water, the products are a gas called _____ and a metal compound called a _____.

# C2.18  Adding non-metals to the reactivity series

Even though they are **non-metals**, we can find places in the reactivity series for hydrogen and carbon.

## Hydrogen

Magnesium displaces hydrogen from steam. So hydrogen will be below magnesium in the reactivity series.

Sodium and calcium both react well with cold water but sodium reacts better. Magnesium reacts very slowly with cold water but reacts more quickly if heated in steam. Zinc reacts more slowly than magnesium if heated in steam and iron reacts more slowly than zinc. Copper doesn't react with steam at all.

1  Write a word equation for the reaction between zinc and water (steam).

2  Write a reactivity series for the metals mentioned above, putting hydrogen in its correct place in the series.

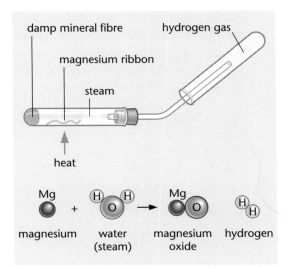

*So hydrogen will be below magnesium in the reactivity series.*

## Carbon

We can find a place for **carbon** in the reactivity series by comparing its attraction for oxygen with the six metals.

The reaction shown in the diagram tells us that carbon has a greater attraction for the oxygen than the lead has because it has taken the oxygen from the lead oxide.

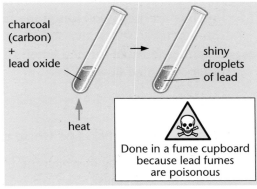

*After heating for some time, shiny droplets of lead are found at the bottom of the test tube*

3  Carbon reacts in a similar way with iron oxide and zinc oxide but cannot take the oxygen from magnesium oxide.

Write a word equation for the reaction of carbon with iron oxide.

4  Write out a reactivity series for the metals mentioned on this page, putting carbon and hydrogen in their correct places.

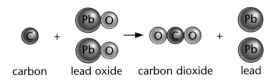

**WHAT YOU NEED TO REMEMBER**  (Copy and complete using the **key words**)

**Adding non-metals to the reactivity series**

We can include hydrogen and _____ in the reactivity series for the metals even though they are _____.

Follows on from: 5.1, 5.2

# C3.1   Different kinds of rocks

example    example    example

granite    chalk    quartzite

igneous    sedimentary    metamorphic

Another one for the metamorphic pile.

Rocks make up the ground we walk on. They make up the crust of the Earth and all its hills and mountains. They make up every single pebble that we find on the beach. Even the tiny grains of sand came from rocks that have been broken up.

There are thousands of different types of rock. To help us to think about all these different rocks, we divide them into groups.

**1 (a)** Look at the picture. Then write down the three groups that scientists sort rocks into.

**(b)** Write one example for each group.

basalt – fast cooling. (you can only see the shape and colour of the tiny crystals under a microscope)

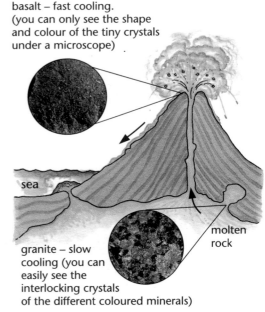

■ **Igneous rocks**

'Igneous' in the Greek language means 'fire'. **Igneous** rocks were once so hot that they were molten. The rocks formed when this molten material cooled down.

Basalt and granite are both igneous rocks.

**2** What are igneous rocks and where are they made?

**3** Write down <u>one</u> way in which the crystals in basalt and granite are similar.

**4 (a)** Write down <u>one</u> way that basalt and granite look different.

**(b)** Which one cooled down quickly and which one cooled down slowly?

sea

molten rock

granite – slow cooling (you can easily see the interlocking crystals of the different coloured minerals)

*The longer the rocks take to solidify, the bigger the crystals are.*

■ **Sedimentary rocks**

**Sedimentary** rocks start off with bits of mud, sand and shells, falling to the bottom of the sea or a lake.

**5** What do we call the bits which settle out?

particles of sediment falling down

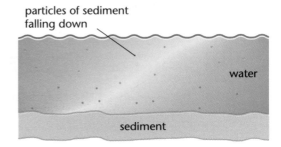

water

sediment

Each layer of sediment gets covered up by new **layers**. As more layers settle on top, the pressure on the lower layers increases. Minerals from the water stick the bits together, so we call it the cement.

**6** Which of the three rocks was made from:

**(a)** animal remains? **(b)** sand grains?

sandstone – a cement holds the sand grains together

chalk

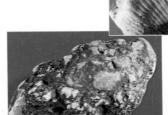

## Metamorphic rocks

When rocks are heated and put under pressure, they slowly change. This happens deep inside the Earth's crust. It takes hundreds of thousands of years. The changed rocks are called **metamorphic** rocks.

conglomerate

*Sedimentary rocks.*

**7** Look at the pictures. Then copy and complete the table.

| Sedimentary rock | Metamorphic rock | How the rock has been changed |
|---|---|---|
| limestone | | |
| | slate | |

Heat and pressure →

limestone          marble

**8** Why are sapphires and rubies so expensive?

 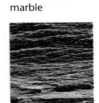

Heat and pressure →

mudstone          slate

*Heat and pressure makes aluminium and oxygen, contained in some rocks, turn into sapphires and rubies. This happens only very rarely.*

*In some metamorphic rocks we can see bands of dark and light crystals.*

These metamorphic rocks are harder and denser than the sedimentary rocks they are made from.

**WHAT YOU NEED TO REMEMBER** (Copy and complete using the **key words**)

**Different kinds of rocks**

When molten rock cools down _____ rocks are formed.

_____ rocks form at the bottom of lakes and seas.
They are made up of sediment that builds up in _____.

Heat and pressure can change rocks. We call the new rocks _____ rocks.

**More about rocks: CORE+ C3.9**

145

# C3.2 Heating up the rock cycle

We don't normally think about rocks moving around. But over millions of years, they do. The centre of the Earth is hot. This energy makes the rocks move around and go through a series of changes. We call this the **rock cycle**.

Weathering breaks up the surface rocks.

Magma rapidly solidifies to form basalt (an igneous rock).

Bits of rock are swept down to the sea.

Magma slowly crystallises to form granite (an igneous rock).

Sedimentary rock forms.

Heat and pressure changes rocks.

metamorphic rock

magma (molten rock)

**1** Copy and complete the rock cycle below.

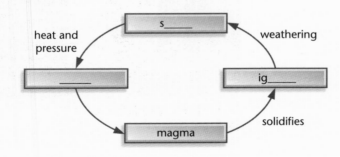

heat and pressure

s_____

weathering

_____

ig_____

magma

solidifies

## ■ The rock cycle and the weather

Most of the energy in the rock cycle comes from under the Earth's crust. But the **weather** also plays a big part in breaking down rocks on the top of the Earth's crust.

**2** Write down <u>four</u> different kinds of weather that can break down rocks.

*Frost, wind, rain and the Sun all play a part in breaking down rocks.*

## Why is it hot inside the Earth?

When the Earth first formed, it was very cold. But **radioactive** substances in the rocks released a tremendous amount of thermal energy. This melted most of the rocks. These molten rocks (magma) make up a layer called the **mantle**.

Thousands of millions of years later, radioactive substances are still releasing energy. So the centre of the Earth is still very **hot**. On the outside is a **crust** of solid rock.

3 Copy the diagram of the Earth. Replace the labels on the diagram with:

    crust   iron and nickel   mantle

4 At the bottom of the deepest hole drilled into the Earth's crust, the temperature is 246°C. Explain why the temperature is a lot higher than at the Earth's surface.

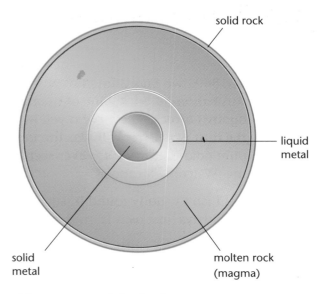

solid rock

liquid metal

solid metal

molten rock (magma)

*The structure of the Earth.*

## Free hot water

In some places, water trickles down to hot rocks in the Earth's crust. Some water changes to steam. This forces hot water back to the surface.

5 Look at the photographs. Then copy and complete the sentences.

Water heated by hot rocks can make _____ and _____ springs.

*A geyser is a mixture of steam and boiling water. In Iceland people use this <u>geothermal</u> energy to heat their homes and provide hot water.*

*The water in this lake comes from a thermal spring.*

### WHAT YOU NEED TO REMEMBER (Copy and complete using the **key words**)

**Heating up the rock cycle**

We live on the Earth's _____.

As we go deeper into the Earth's crust, it gets very _____.

Between the crust and the core, there is a layer of molten rock (magma) called the _____.

Rocks slowly move around all the time. We call this the _____ _____.
The energy for this movement comes from _____ substances and from the _____.

**More about the rock cycle: CORE+ C3.9**

Follows on from: 5.7

# C3.3  Getting metals out of rocks

In 1869, two Englishmen were walking in the Australian outback. One of them stubbed his toe against a rock. They saw a yellow gleam through the dust on the rock. It was the largest nugget of pure gold the world has ever seen. They called it the 'Welcome Stranger'.

Gold isn't usually found in such large pieces. But it's always 'just as it is' in the ground.

We call gold a **native** metal.

**1**  Why was gold one of the very first metals to be used by humans?

**2**  What does the nugget's age tell you about how reactive gold is?

## Other native metals

We sometimes find other unreactive metals in the ground as native metals. But getting these metals from the ground is usually very hard work.

| Metals that we find native |
| --- |
| copper |
| mercury |
| silver |
| platinum |
| gold                   least reactive |

**3**  What metals do we sometimes find native?

**4**  Why is getting the gold from the ground usually very hard work?

## Metals and ores

We find most metals joined to other elements as compounds. Rocks containing metals or metal compounds are called **ores**.

Early people found very little copper as a native metal. But they did discover that heating certain rocks in a charcoal fire gave copper.

**REMEMBER** from page 126

Most metals corrode because they react with other substances such as oxygen. Metals which don't corrode are very unreactive.

The 'Welcome Stranger' weighed about 71 kg and contained 70 kg of pure gold. The gold in the nugget was millions of years old.

In the gold mines of South Africa, there are only about 14 grams of gold per tonne of crushed rock.

native copper

5 (a) What does copper look like?

(b) What does the copper ore called malachite look like?

(c) Can you see any actual copper metal in the copper ore? Explain your answer.

*Malachite is an ore for copper because it contains copper carbonate.*

## Getting metals from their ores

When you heat copper ore with charcoal (carbon) you get copper metal. A new substance is produced so there has been a <u>chemical</u> change. A chemical <u>reaction</u> has happened.

When we use a chemical reaction to get a metal out of its ore, we call this **smelting**.

Most iron ores contain iron joined with oxygen. To get the iron, we need to remove the oxygen. It is much harder to get iron out of its ore than copper. It needs a higher temperature. So we heat coke (carbon) and iron oxide in a **blast furnace**.

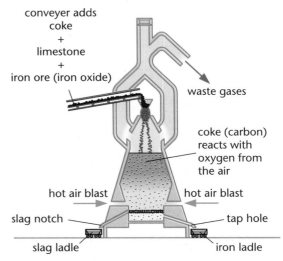

6 What makes the high temperature of the blast furnace?

Metals above **carbon** in the reactivity series cannot easily be separated from their ores by heating with carbon, even at very high temperatures. This is why many metals were not discovered until scientists could split up metal compounds using **electricity**.

7 Name a metal that might be smelted using electricity.

### Reactivity series of some metals

sodium           most reactive
magnesium
aluminium
carbon (a non-metal)
zinc
iron
lead
copper
gold          least reactive

---

**WHAT YOU NEED TO REMEMBER** (Copy and complete using the **key words**)

### Getting metals out of rocks

A metal found in the ground as itself is said to be _____.
Rocks that contain metals or metal compounds are called _____.

When we use a chemical reaction to get a metal out of its ore, we call this _____.
We smelt iron in a _____ _____.

More reactive metals cannot be got from their ores by heating with _____
so they are smelted using _____.

**More about smelting: CORE+ C3.10**

149

Follows on from: 5.8

# C3.4  Corroding metals

If a metal is more reactive, it is harder to get it out of its ore. But that's not the only problem. If a metal is more reactive, it will react faster with substances such as oxygen. We call this **corrosion**.

1  Look at the photograph. Why do archaeologists hardly ever find complete Viking swords?

*This Viking sword is about a thousand years old. It is very rare. Archaeologists usually only find the wooden handles of Viking swords.*

## ■ Rusting and the motor car

The average life of a motor car in the UK used to be only about seven years. After that, most cars were so rusty they were fit only for scrap.

Rusting takes place when iron or steel is in contact with both air and **water**. Rusting is an example of what we call corrosion.

Look at the photograph of the car exported to California soon after it was made.

Compare it with the photograph of the car that stayed in Britain.

2  (a)  Which vehicle shows the most rusting?

   (b)  Write down a reason why this is so.

*This car was exported to California soon after it was made. The climate there is warm and dry.*

## ■ How can rusting be prevented?

Most ways of slowing rusting down put some kind of **barrier** between the iron and the air and water.

3  Explain what the barrier is in each of these pictures.

*This photograph shows a close up of a car made in the same year but which stayed in Britain.*

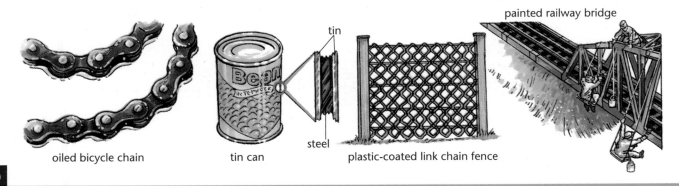

oiled bicycle chain          tin can          plastic-coated link chain fence          painted railway bridge

**4** If there is a break in the tin coating, the steel that is exposed to air and water rusts more quickly than usual.

How is this different from what happens with zinc coating?

## Improving the barrier

One of the best ways of preventing steel from rusting is to coat the steel with **zinc**. We call this galvanised steel. Galvanising steel makes it more expensive.

Look at the table. It shows the guarantees modern cars carry against rusting.

**5** Why do cars last longer now than in the 1960s?

**6** What makes the guarantees different?

**7** Why aren't all the steel parts of all cars galvanised?

*A coating of zinc is better than paint or plastic.*
It protects the steel even when there is a scratch in the coating.

| Make of car | Percentage of galvanised steel in car body | Anti-rusting guarantee in years |
|---|---|---|
| A | 100 | 10 |
| B | 50 | 6 |
| C | 35 | 5 |
| D | 70 | 8 |

## Corrosion of other metals

The less reactive a metal is, the less likely it is to **corrode** or tarnish.

Look at the pictures of gold and silver.

**8** What does the picture tell you about gold? Give a reason for your answer.

**9** What does the picture tell you about silver?

**10** Which of these two metals is more reactive, silver or gold? Explain your answer.

*This gold wedding ring has been in and out of water 'lots of times' every day for thirty years.*

some weeks later

silver goblet

---

**WHAT YOU NEED TO REMEMBER** (Copy and complete using the **key words**)

**Corroding metals**

Rusting is a special case of _____.
Rusting takes place when iron or steel is in contact with both air and _____.

Most methods of slowing down rusting use a _____.
One of the best barriers is _____.

The less reactive a metal is, the less likely it is to _____.

Follows on from: 4.2, 4.3

# C3.5 Acids and alkalis

Acids are often made in the air. For example, whenever a volcano erupts, it throws tonnes of **acidic** gases into the air.

Whenever lightning flashes, the energy from the flash makes oxygen and nitrogen from the air react. This produces acidic gases called <u>nitrogen oxides</u>.

**1** Look at the diagrams. Then copy and complete the table.

|  | Acidic gas produced | Acid produced |
|---|---|---|
| volcanoes |  |  |
| lightning |  |  |

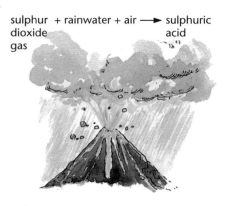

sulphur + rainwater + air ⟶ sulphuric
dioxide                         acid
gas

nitrogen + oxygen + water ⟶ nitric acid

## Alkalis

The opposites of acids are **alkalis**. These are not as common as acids. But we can easily make alkalis from two substances we find in the Earth's crust.

**2** What alkaline substance is made:

(a) from salt?

(b) by heating limestone?

(c) from both salt and limestone?

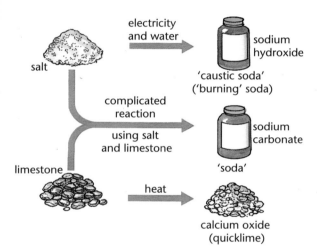

salt

electricity and water ⟶ sodium hydroxide
'caustic soda' ('burning' soda)

complicated reaction
using salt and limestone ⟶ sodium carbonate
'soda'

limestone

heat ⟶ calcium oxide (quicklime)

## Making useful substances from alkalis

Alkalis are very useful.

Early houses had only very primitive windows. For example, the Romans used very thin leather smeared with oil.

**3** Roman windows were good for some purposes but not for others. Explain why.

**4 (a)** What material do we use now for windows?

**(b)** What alkaline substances are used to make this material?

*Roman windows let light through, but you could not see through them clearly.*

sand + quicklime + soda ⟶ furnace ⟶ glass

### More things made from alkalis

Until the 19th century, people made soap by boiling fat with wood ashes. Soap was very expensive. So most people did not wash themselves with soap very often.

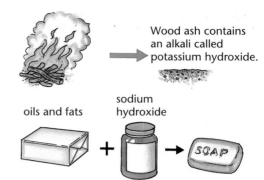
Wood ash contains an alkali called potassium hydroxide.

**5 (a)** Why were wood ashes used to make soap?

**(b)** What alkali do we use today to make soap?

oils and fats    sodium hydroxide    SOAP

*How we make soap today.*

People have used natural fibres like wool, cotton, silk and linen for thousands of years. Rayon was the first artificial fibre.

**6** What alkali do we use to make it?

wood chips    sodium hydroxide    rayon

*How rayon is made.*

### Acidic, neutral or alkaline?

Many plants contain natural **dyes** that change **colour** in acids and alkalis. Chemists call these dyes, **indicators**. They tell us whether a substance is acidic or alkaline. They can also tell us whether a substance is <u>neutral</u>.

**7** Why are the flowers in the photographs different colours?

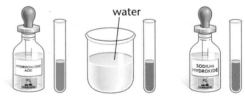
More acidic soil    …less acidic soil

### Litmus

Litmus is a very well known indicator that comes from a kind of plant called a lichen.

**8** What colour is litmus with:

**(a)** acids?  **(b)** alkalis?  **(c)** neutral solutions?

water

*The test tubes contain litmus mixed with each of the other substances.*

---

**WHAT YOU NEED TO REMEMBER** (Copy and complete using the **key words**)

**Acids and alkalis**

Sulphur dioxide from volcanoes and nitrogen oxides from lightning are _____ gases.

The opposites of acids are _____.

Chemists tell the difference between acids and alkalis by using _____.
These are often natural _____. In acids and alkalis, they change _____.

Follows on from: 4.4, 4.5

# C3.6 Acids in the soil

For farmers and gardeners, the most important part of the Earth's crust is the layer of soil on the top.

They sometimes test the soil with a special indicator called <u>universal indicator</u>.

This tells them more than just whether the soil is acidic or alkaline. It also tells them <u>how</u> acidic or alkaline it is.

The indicator measures **pH** (said 'pea-aitch').

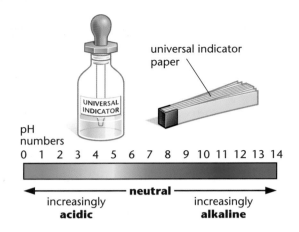

1 Copy and complete the following.

_____ pH numbers = more acidic
_____ pH numbers = more alkaline
A pH number of 7 = _____

| Crop | Best pH for plant |
|---|---|
| potatoes | 5 |
| peas | 5.5 |
| maize | 6 |
| sugar beet | 6.5 |
| cabbage | 7–8 |

## ■ Getting rid of soil acidity

When soil is too acidic, many plants will not grow. Some plants, such as cabbages, grow better in slightly alkaline soil. Gardeners add slaked lime (calcium hydroxide) to their soil. Slaked lime is an alkali. This neutralises or takes away the acid in the soil.

2 Farmer Giles wants to plant potatoes, peas, sugar beet, maize and cabbages.

Copy the plan of the farm and write what he should plant on each field.

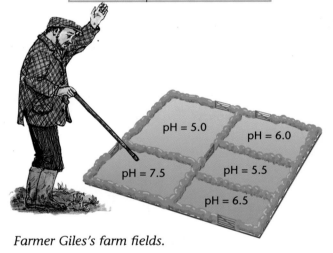

*Farmer Giles's farm fields.*

## ■ Using fertilisers

Adding fertilisers to the soil helps plants like wheat to grow.

3 What happens to the acidity of the soil if the farmer uses fertilisers year after year?

4 Farmers using fertilisers need to add slaked lime to the fields. Explain why.

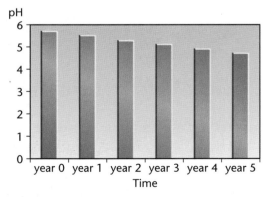

*How using fertiliser for several years affects the acidity of soil.*

# What new substances does neutralisation make?

Neutralisations are chemical reactions. Like all chemical reactions, they make new substances.

When an alkali neutralises an acid, we get a **salt** and **water**.

5 The diagram shows an experiment where sodium hydroxide was added to hydrochloric acid drop by drop.

(a) Write down the pH in each flask. [Use the chart opposite.]

(b) Which flask shows the end of the neutralisation reaction?

(c) What <u>two</u> substances does the reaction make?

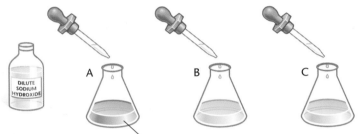

dilute hydrochloric acid plus universal indicator

*The salt produced in the reaction between this acid and this alkali is called sodium chloride.*

# Another way to neutralise soil

Farmers can also neutralise the soil in their fields by spreading crushed limestone on it.

Limestone is calcium carbonate. When a carbonate neutralises an acid, you get a salt, water and **carbon dioxide** gas.

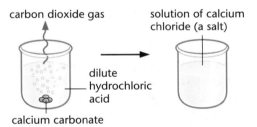

carbon dioxide gas

solution of calcium chloride (a salt)

dilute hydrochloric acid

calcium carbonate

*All metal carbonates react with acid in the same way as calcium carbonate.*

6 Copy and complete the word equation for this reaction.

_____ acid + calcium _____ → calcium _____ + _____ + _____ _____

---

**WHAT YOU NEED TO REMEMBER** (Copy and complete using the **key words**)

**Acids in the soil**

We use universal indicator to measure _____.
A pH of 7 means that the solution is _____.

When the pH is less than 7, we have an _____ solution.
When the pH is more than 7, we have an _____ solution.

When an alkali neutralises an acid, we get a _____ and _____ only.
When a carbonate neutralises an acid, we get a salt, water and _____ _____.

**More about salts: CORE+ C3.11**

# C3.7 Weathering rocks

Gold miners in ancient Egypt needed to break up rocks to get the gold. So they built fires to heat up the rock faces deep inside the mines. The rock expanded. They then threw cold water on to the hot rock. The rock cooled suddenly, contracted and shattered. The miners could then get at the bits of gold in the rock.

Something similar happens in deserts.

1 What happens to the stones of the gibber deserts

   (a) during the day?  (b) at night?

2 Explain how the Egyptain gold miners were 'imitating nature'.

*Imitating nature in an ancient Egyptian gold mine.*

*Australian gibber plains. The stones range from about 30 cm across down to small pebbles. The Sun's heat causes them to expand and the cold of the night causes them to contract. This cracks the stones into smaller and smaller pebbles.*

## ■ Wind

When the **wind** blows hard in a desert, it makes a sandstorm. When bits of sand hit the surface of a rock, they gradually wear it away. We say that they <u>scour</u> away the rock.

3 Why is the rock in the picture shaped like a mushroom?

*In sandstorms, the air close to the ground contains the most sand. So this air scours the rock most.*

## ■ Water

Water gets into cracks in the rocks. When the temperature drops, the water freezes. Water expands when it freezes. This can force a crack to become wider and wider. Eventually the rock splits.

Water rushing down a mountainside carries with it small bits of rock. These grind away at other rocks, wearing them down.

4 A large rock from the top of a mountain can eventually end up as a lot of small rounded pebbles at the bottom of the mountain. Describe how this happens.

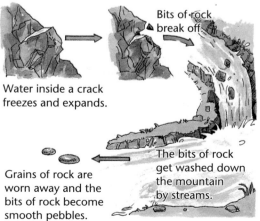

Water inside a crack freezes and expands.

Bits of rock break off.

The bits of rock get washed down the mountain by streams.

Grains of rock are worn away and the bits of rock become smooth pebbles.

## ■ Rivers of ice

In cold climates, huge rivers of **ice** flow down mountains. These are called <u>glaciers</u>. The huge weight of the ice grinds away at the rock.

5 If a glacier moved at about two metres a year, how long would it take to travel 1 kilometre?

It is the weather that causes the surfaces of rocks to break up. We call this **physical weathering**. The wind, water and ice break down the rocks into smaller pieces and carry them away. This is called erosion. The Sun also helps to break down rocks.

*Glaciers contain millions of tonnes of ice. They slide down at a few metres per year. They carve out entire valleys. They carry thousands of tonnes of ground up rocks with them.*

## ■ Chemical weathering

Carbon dioxide dissolves in rainwater to make it slightly acidic. Rainwater very slowly reacts with rocks that contain carbonates. We call this **chemical weathering**.

6 Is the chemical weathering of limestone a fast or slow process? Explain your answer.

Chemical weathering takes place faster when the air is polluted with other acidic gases. These are mainly sulphur dioxide and nitrogen oxides from burning fuels.

*This is known as a limestone pavement. Every 500 years, the rainwater dissolves another 1 cm of limestone. The rainwater reacts chemically with the limestone. The new substance formed dissolves in the water. The gaps between the slabs become deeper as the rainwater drains through them.*

7 (a) Where is the air more polluted with acidic gases – in the countryside or in the town?

(b) Why are the surfaces of some buildings in towns badly worn away?

*Motor vehicles produce acidic gases.*

---

**WHAT YOU NEED TO REMEMBER** (Copy and complete using the **key words**)

**Weathering rocks**

Rocks are broken down into smaller pieces by the Sun, the_____, water and _____ This is called _____ _____ .

Chemical reactions can also attack rocks. We call this _____ _____

**More about ice and water: CORE+ C3.12, C3.13**

157

# C3.8 Looking after the environment

*An industrial town in the 1950s.*

We live on top of the Earth's crust. But this is only part of our environment. The air in the Earth's atmosphere and the water in rivers, lakes and seas, are also part of our environment. How we live and what we do also affects these parts of our environment.

The air and the water in our environment have improved in some ways over the last 40 years. The air is cleaner because coal is no longer burnt in most homes and factories. Our rivers and streams are cleaner because we now try to stop factories and sewage works from discharging waste straight into the waterways.

**1** How did many ordinary people pollute the air before the 1960s?

**2** How did factories damage the environment?

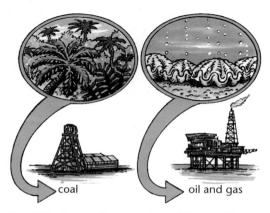

coal        oil and gas

*Fossil fuels are the remains of living things. These remains are found underground. They were changed by heat and pressure into what they are now – coal, gas or oil.*

## ■ Using fossil fuels

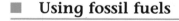

Fossil fuels are our main source of **energy**.

**3 (a)** Write down <u>three</u> fossil fuels.

**(b)** Why are they called fossil fuels?

Each of the pictures shows a fossil fuel (or a fuel made from a fossil fuel) being used.

**4** Give <u>one</u> example of how each of these fuels is used:

coal     petrol     diesel     gas     wax

All these fuels contain carbon and **hydrogen**.

**5** When petrol burns, what new <u>substances</u> do the following make?

**(a)** carbon atoms     **(b)** hydrogen atoms

**6** What else do these burning fuels release?

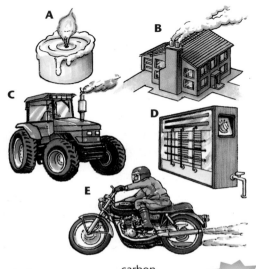

petrol + oxygen ⟶ carbon dioxide + water + energy

## ■ Pollution from cars

The invention of the motor car was one of the biggest changes that happened in the last 100 years. Cars give us a freedom to travel around.

**7** What is the main difference between the two photographs of the same street?

**8** What does the graph tell us about the use of the motor car?

When a car burns petrol or diesel, it doesn't only produce carbon dioxide and **water**. It also makes small amounts of poisonous gases such as carbon monoxide and **nitrogen oxides**. Diesel engines also give out smoke containing carbon particles that enter deep into our lungs. All of this pollution can damage our health.

Car engines and exhausts are being improved all the time to reduce the amount of pollution they cause. But the number of cars keeps on increasing.

**9** Will the pollution from cars get worse or get better? Explain your answer.

*The Strand, London, in 1887.*

*The Strand, London, in the 1990s.*

*Forecast of car ownership in Britain to 2020.*

## ■ Controlling a burning fuel

For burning to take place, three things must be present. We can show this in what is called the <u>fire triangle</u>.

**10** Look at the fire triangle. Write down <u>three</u> ways in which a fire can be put out.

*The fire triangle has three sides. Take away one of the sides, and the triangle collapses and the fire goes out.*

fuel · air (oxygen) · heat

---

**WHAT YOU NEED TO REMEMBER** (Copy and complete using the **key words**)

**Looking after the environment**

Fossil fuels contain carbon and _____.
When fossil fuels or fuels made from fossil fuels burn, they produce carbon dioxide and _____.
The useful thing that we get from fossil fuels is _____.

The motor car also produces small amounts of carbon monoxide and

_____ _____.

**More about pollution: CORE+ C3.14, C3.15**

# C3.9  More about the rock cycle

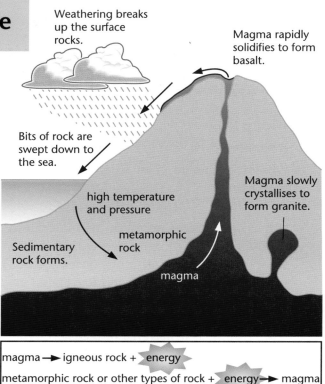

Weathering breaks up the surface rocks.

Magma rapidly solidifies to form basalt.

Bits of rock are swept down to the sea.

high temperature and pressure

metamorphic rock

Sedimentary rock forms.

magma

Magma slowly crystallises to form granite.

magma → igneous rock + energy

metamorphic rock or other types of rock + energy → magma

The diagram shows you what you already know about the rock cycle.

If rock gets very hot, it may melt and form magma.

**1** Does this change take in or give out energy?

When magma solidifies, it forms igneous rock.

**2** Does this change take in or give out energy?

But there are some things that this simple rock cycle diagram doesn't explain. For example, the rocks at the tops of very high mountains are often **sedimentary** rocks.

**3** Why can't the rock cycle diagram explain this?

*This rock from the top of a mountain contains fossils. So it must be a sedimentary rock.*

## ■ How do sedimentary rocks get to the tops of mountains?

The Earth's crust is split into different sections or 'plates'. These plates float around on the hot, liquid magma beneath.

When two plates collide, one of them can be pushed up to form **mountains**.

**4 (a)** What type of rocks do we sometimes find at the top of mountains?

**(b)** Explain how the fossils came to be in the rock.

**5** How did sedimentary rocks get to the top of mountains?

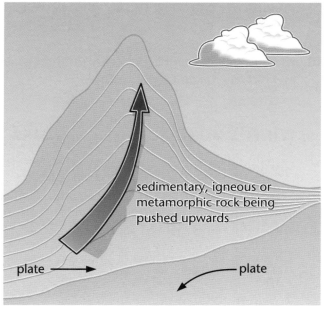

sedimentary, igneous or metamorphic rock being pushed upwards

plate

plate

## ■ Making more sedimentary rocks

All types of rock can be pushed up to form new mountains. These rocks are gradually broken down and eventually form new sedimentary rocks.

The diagrams show how.

**6** Copy and complete the flow chart below. Use the information from the diagrams to help you.

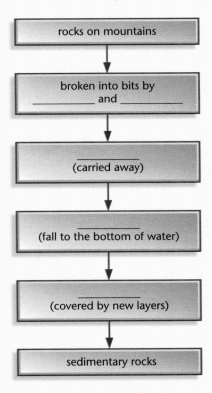

```
┌─────────────────────────────┐
│      rocks on mountains      │
└─────────────────────────────┘
              ↓
┌─────────────────────────────┐
│      broken into bits by     │
│      _____ and _____   │
└─────────────────────────────┘
              ↓
┌─────────────────────────────┐
│         _____             │
│        (carried away)        │
└─────────────────────────────┘
              ↓
┌─────────────────────────────┐
│         _____             │
│   (fall to the bottom of water) │
└─────────────────────────────┘
              ↓
┌─────────────────────────────┐
│         _____             │
│     (covered by new layers)  │
└─────────────────────────────┘
              ↓
┌─────────────────────────────┐
│       sedimentary rocks      │
└─────────────────────────────┘
```

**7** Write down <u>three</u> ways in which rocks are transported down a mountain.

*Rocks are broken into bits by **weathering** and **erosion**.*

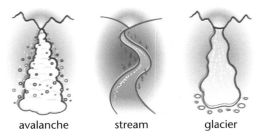

avalanche        stream        glacier

*Small bits of rock are carried down mountains. This is called **transportation**.*

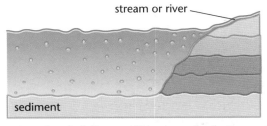

stream or river

sediment

*Bits of rock fall as sediment to the bottom of lakes and sea. This is called **deposition**.*

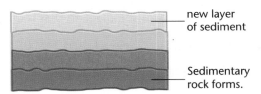

new layer of sediment

Sedimentary rock forms.

*Old layers of sediment are covered by new layers. This is called **burial**.*

---

**WHAT YOU NEED TO REMEMBER** (Copy and complete using the **key words**)

**More about the rock cycle**

When plates in the Earth's crust collide, rocks are slowly pushed up to form _____.

The rocks at the top of the new mountain can be igneous, metamorphic or _____.
These rocks are then broken down by _____ and _____.
They are carried down the mountainside; this is called _____.
When bits of rock reach a lake or the sea they form a sediment; this is called _____.
Later new rock is formed as the sediment gets covered up; this is called _____.

# C3.10 Smelting metals

Look at the formulas of the ores in the box.

**1 (a)** Which metals do these two ores contain?

**(b)** What do these two ores have in common?

### ■ How easy is it to smelt a metal?

To get a metal out of one of its compounds, we have to remove the non-metals. This needs energy. The more **reactive** the metal is, then the more **energy** we must put in to extract each atom of the metal.

**2** To extract the same number of atoms of metal, which ore needs the most energy, $Fe_2O_3$ or $Al_2O_3$? Explain your answer.

To extract iron from iron oxide, we heat it in a blast furnace with **carbon** (coke).

### Reactions in a blast furnace

carbon + oxygen → carbon dioxide + energy

carbon dioxide + carbon → carbon monoxide

carbon monoxide + iron oxide → iron + carbon dioxide

**3 (a)** Write down the reaction that provides the energy.

**(b)** Write down the reaction that is a <u>reduction</u> reaction.

### ■ Extracting aluminium

**4** Aluminium is the most common metal in the Earth's crust. But it was not extracted until 1827. What does this tell you about aluminium?

We use **electricity** to get aluminium.

### The chemical formula of an ore tells you:
■ what elements are in the chemical compound;
■ how many atoms of each element are in the formula.
$Fe_2O_3$ contains 2 atoms of iron for every 3 atoms of oxygen, and $Al_2O_3$ contains 2 atoms of aluminium for every 3 atoms of oxygen.

### Reactivity series of metals

| | |
|---|---|
| sodium | most reactive |
| magnesium | extracted with |
| aluminium | electricity |
| zinc | |
| iron | can be extracted |
| lead | with carbon |
| copper | |
| silver | found native |
| gold | least reactive |

Removing oxygen from a compound is a <u>reduction</u> reaction.

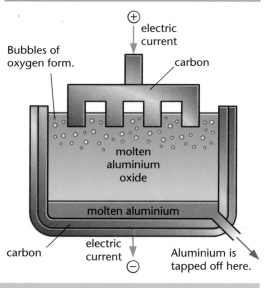

### WHAT YOU NEED TO REMEMBER (Copy and complete using the **key words**)

**Smelting metals**

The more _____ the metal, the more _____ is needed to extract it.
We smelt metals in the middle of the reactivity series, like iron, with _____.
But for metals higher in the reactivity series, like aluminium, we use _____.

# C3.11 More about salts

When an acid and an alkali react together, they make a salt and water.

1 Look at the word equation.

(a) What salt is produced in this reaction?

(b) What kind of reaction is it?

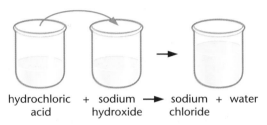

hydrochloric + sodium ⟶ sodium + water
acid          hydroxide    chloride

*In a salt, you always put the name of the metal first.*

## ■ Making different salts

The type of salt you get in a reaction depends on what acid and what alkali you use.

2 What salt do you get when the following react together?

(a) nitric acid and sodium hydroxide

(b) sulphuric acid and potassium hydroxide

**Which acid? Which salt?**

Hydrochloric acid makes **chlorides**.

Nitric acid makes **nitrates**.

Sulphuric acid makes **sulphates**.

## ■ Another way to make salts

A reactive metal can displace hydrogen from acids. This word equation shows the reaction between magnesium and sulphuric acid to make the salt magnesium sulphate.

magnesium + sulphuric → magnesium + hydrogen
              acid            sulphate

3 Write a word equation to show the reaction of:

(a) zinc with sulphuric acid.

(b) magnesium with hydrochloric acid.

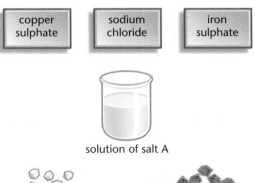

| copper sulphate | sodium chloride | iron sulphate |

solution of salt A

## ■ Looking at salts

Iron salts are usually pale green or yellow. Copper salts are usually blue. Most other salts are white.

4 Look at the pictures. Match the labels with the salts A, B and C.

crystals of salt B          crystals of salt C

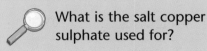
What is the salt copper sulphate used for?

---

**WHAT YOU NEED TO REMEMBER** (Copy and complete using the **key words**)

**More about salts**

Hydrochloric acid makes salts called _____. Sulphuric acid makes salts called _____.
Nitric acid makes salts called _____.

# C3.12 Why are ice and water so strange?

Water is the most common liquid on Earth. But from a scientific point of view, water is very strange.

Most liquids get smaller or contract when they turn into a solid. But water gets bigger or **expands** when it freezes.

1  What happens to water pipes:

   (a)  when the water freezes?

   (b)  when the frozen pipes thaw?

2  Freezing water exerts a large push force. Write down another example of where this force is important.

water in crack

one rock   freezing weather   two rocks

## ■ The water model

Look at the diagrams of water molecules (particles) in water and ice.

3  (a)  Describe what happens when water freezes. Use the words <u>molecules</u> and <u>expands</u> in your answer.

   (b)  What usually happens to the particles of a substance when it freezes?

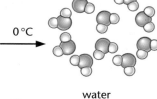

0 °C

liquid water

single water molecule

water as ice

*In ice, the molecules are slightly **further away** from each other than in water.*

## ■ Icebergs

Look at the photograph.

4  (a)  Use the idea of the distance between molecules to explain why ice floats on water.

   (b)  Water has a density of 1 g/cm$^3$. The volume of a sheet of ice is 1000 cm$^3$.
   If the mass of the ice is 900 g, what is the density of ice?
   (Remember: density = $\frac{mass}{volume}$ )

*Ice is less **dense** than water.*

## WHAT YOU NEED TO REMEMBER (Copy and complete using the **key words**)

**Why are ice and water are so strange?**

When water freezes, it _____.
This means that the molecules in ice are _____ _____ from each other than the molecules in water.
This is why ice is less _____ than water.

# C3.13 Why do some rocks dissolve?

Rain dissolves some gases from the air. One of these gases is carbon dioxide.

This solution of carbon dioxide in water is a very weak **acid**. It reacts with rocks that contain calcium carbonate.

Calcium carbonate is not affected by pure water. But with carbon dioxide present, a very slow reaction takes place.

**1** What new substance is formed?

**Calcium bicarbonate** is soluble in water. So the rock slowly **dissolves**.

**2** Caves and potholes are common in limestone areas. Explain why.

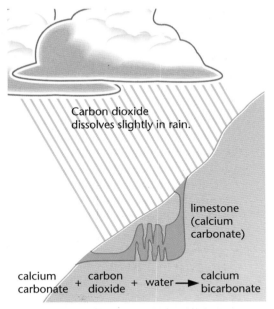

Carbon dioxide dissolves slightly in rain.

limestone (calcium carbonate)

calcium carbonate + carbon dioxide + water ⟶ calcium bicarbonate

## Stalactites and stalagmites

Calcium bicarbonate can only exist in solution. When drips of water fall from the roof of a limestone cave, some of the water evaporates. The previous reaction is reversed. The calcium bicarbonate breaks down and leaves a few microscopic specks of calcium carbonate behind. These build up over thousands of years into a stalactite.

When a drip of water splashes on to the floor of the cave, a similar reaction happens, and a stalagmite forms.

**3** How long would it take a stalactite to grow 4 centimetres?

**4** Write a word equation for the formation of stalactites and stalagmites.

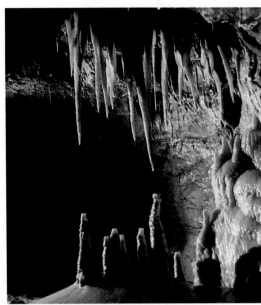

*A typical stalactite grows at about 8 mm per year.*

---

**WHAT YOU NEED TO REMEMBER** (Copy and complete using the **key words**)

**Why do some rocks dissolve?**

Carbon dioxide dissolves in water to make a very weak _____.
This reacts with calcium carbonate rocks to make a soluble substance called _____ _____.
So the rock slowly _____.

# C3.14 Carbon dioxide and the greenhouse effect

Go into a greenhouse on a cold winter's day and you could be pleasantly surprised. The temperature is almost always warmer than outside. The diagram shows why.

**1** How does the greenhouse stay warmer inside than outside?

Some gases in the atmosphere – **carbon dioxide** and methane – act like the glass of the greenhouse. They let the heat rays from the Sun pass through. But they absorb the longer wave heat rays given off by the Earth and send some of that heat back to Earth.

**2** How does the greenhouse effect work for the Earth?

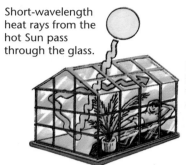

Short-wavelength heat rays from the hot Sun pass through the glass.

Long-wavelength heat rays from the greenhouse cannot escape.

The atmosphere includes carbon dioxide and methane.

surface of the Earth

## ■ Level of carbon dioxide in the atmosphere

Until about 150 years ago, there was about 0.03% of carbon dioxide in the air. This had been roughly the same for millions of years.

But for the last 150 years or so, we have burned **fossil fuels** at an increasing rate. This releases more carbon dioxide into the air. Today, the level of carbon dioxide is about 0.035% and is still rising.

Carbon dioxide doesn't do any harm directly. But with more carbon dioxide in the air, we expect the greenhouse effect to increase. The Earth's average **temperature** may be 1 to 2°C warmer in the near future. This might affect our weather and cause more of the ice at the North and South poles to melt.

**3 (a)** What might happen because of an increased greenhouse effect?

**(b)** Explain how this might happen.

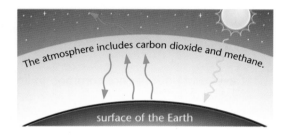

increasing areas of desert

melting of the polar ice

rising sea levels

longer and more frequent famines

*What might happen if the Earth gets warmer.*

## WHAT YOU NEED TO REMEMBER (Copy and complete using the **key words**)

**Carbon dioxide and the greenhouse effect**

One of the greenhouse gases is _____ _____.

The amount of carbon dioxide in the air increases because we burn _____ _____.

An increase in the greenhouse effect will raise the Earth's average _____.

# C3.15  Waste and pollution

Waste produced by all villages, towns and cities doesn't just **disappear**. It has to be got rid of.

1  What happens to the household waste that we put into the dustbin?

2  Where would the waste that we flush down the sewer finish up if it wasn't treated?

 Find out about the things in waste that can be recycled and how they are then re-used.

sewage treatment plant

river

sea

### ■ Waste gases

When we burn waste, it does look as if we've got rid of it altogether. But we haven't really. The diagram shows why.

3  What happens to the waste that seems to disappear when you burn it?

4  Why can't waste ever just disappear?

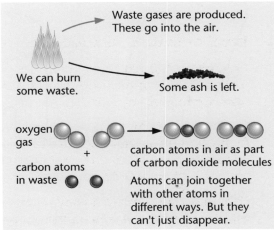

Waste gases are produced. These go into the air.

We can burn some waste.

Some ash is left.

oxygen gas

carbon atoms in waste

+

carbon atoms in air as part of carbon dioxide molecules

Atoms can join together with other atoms in different ways. But they can't just disappear.

### ■ How can we prevent pollution?

All the waste we produce has to go somewhere here on Earth. That's why there's a problem with pollution.

5  Hardly any matter leaves the Earth. What are the only <u>two</u> ways that this can happen?

The only way we can prevent pollution is to change all our waste into **harmless** substances. Then we can let them into the air or put them into the ground or into our rivers, lakes and seas.

*Space rockets move fast enough to escape from Earth. The only other things that can move this fast are hydrogen molecules.*

## WHAT YOU NEED TO REMEMBER  (Copy and complete using the **key words**)

**Waste and pollution**

Waste is a problem because it can never just _____.

To prevent pollution, we must change waste into _____ substances.

# Investigating a candle burning

Science isn't just about what other people have found out. It is also about finding things out for yourself. As you read about how Seema investigates a candle burning you will learn about how to do science.

Seema puts a glass jar over a burning candle.

After six seconds the candle goes out.

Seema thinks that this happens because all the air has gone.

*six seconds later*

## INFORMATION

- Candle wax needs oxygen to burn

- About one-fifth of the air is oxygen

**1** Read the 'Information' box.

Then copy and complete the following.

After six seconds the candle goes _____.
This is because _____
(Answer as fully as you can.)

Seema wonders whether the candle will burn for a longer time if she uses a larger jar.

**2** What do you think will happen?
Give a reason for your answer.

When you say what you think will happen you are making a **prediction**.

Scientists often make predictions.
Then they test their predictions to see if they are right.

## Planning an experiment

To find out whether her prediction is right, Seema must **plan** an experiment.

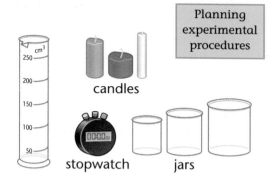

candles

stopwatch    jars

**3** Copy the table. Then complete it to show what Seema should do. (Use the diagram of apparatus to help you.)

| Problem | Plan |
|---|---|
| What can Seema use to measure the number of seconds the candle burns? | |
| What can Seema use to measure how much air there is in each jar (the volume)? | |
| How can Seema keep the experiment fair? | |
| The candle doesn't burn for very long. | |
| How can Seema get an accurate result for how long the candle burns?* | |
| How should Seema record her results?* | |

[* Hint - if you don't know the answers to these questions look at the table below.]

## Seema's results

The table shows the results of Seema's experiment.

| Size of jar | How much air the jar holds (the volume in cm$^3$) | How many seconds the candle burns | | | | |
|---|---|---|---|---|---|---|
| | | 1st. try | 2nd. try | 3rd. try | 4th. try | Average |
| small | 250 | 2 | 3 | 3 | 4 | 3 |
| medium | 500 | 5 | 6 | 7 | 6 | 6 |
| large | 1000 | 13 | 12 | 14 | 13 | 13 |

## What do Seema's results tell us?

Look carefully at Seema's results.

**4** Copy and complete the sentences.

When there is a bigger volume of air the candle burns for a _____ time.
This is/is not what I predicted would happen.

### ■ Drawing a graph

A graph is often a good way to show the measurements you make in an experiment.

You can then <u>see</u> what the results tell you.

5 Plot Seema's results on a graph.
[The diagram shows you how to do this.]
Then draw the graph line.

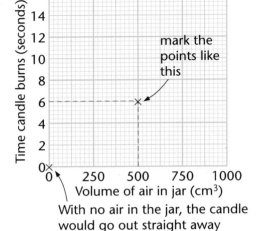

With no air in the jar, the candle would go out straight away

### ■ Testing another idea

Seema has another idea.

She predicts that a fat candle will go out quicker than a thin candle because it will use up the oxygen faster.

She tests her idea using a large jar.

Her results are underneath the diagram.

6 Was Seema's prediction correct?

7 Why do you think the results for the two candles are about the same?

8 Why does Seema get slightly different results even for the <u>same</u> candle?

Seema's teacher told her to cross out two of her measurements (the 0s and the 9s).

9 (a) Why should Seema should ignore these results?

(b) What do you think happened to give each of these bad measurements?

| Time taken for candles to go out (s = seconds) | |
|---|---|
| Fat candle | Thin candle |
| 24 s | 23 s |
| 25 s | 9s |
| 24 s | 25 s |
| 0s | 24 s |
| 25 s | 24 s |

Considering the strength of evidence

## ■ What else could Seema investigate?

Seema's teacher asks the class what other differences between candles might affect the results of the tests.

Here are some of the ideas the pupils come up with:

- ■ the height of the candles

- ■ the wicks of the candles
  (what they are made of, how fat they are)

- ■ the colour of the candles

Differences like these are often called **factors** or **variables**.

**10 (a)** For each of the factors mentioned by the pupils say whether or not you think it will affect how quickly the candle goes out under a jar.

    **(b)** Give a reason for each of your answers.

**11** You have made your predictions.
If you are a good scientist, what should you do next?

# What you need to know about Key Stage 3 Science SATs

Science SATs papers look very long. Don't worry about this. Most pupils have enough time to answer all of the questions.

Easier questions are at the beginning of the paper, but you will be able to answer some, if not all, of most questions. So start with the questions and parts of questions you find easy. Then go back to the more difficult ones.

**Read each question carefully to see what you have to do.**

■ Sometimes you have to choose the right answer from those provided in the question.
Read *all* the possible answers before you choose.

This kind of question comes in several different forms.

■ 'Tick the correct box' means tick *one* box. So don't tick more than one box unless the question tells you to.

This gets 1 mark.

Which of these elements is a metal?

Tick the correct box.

| | |
|---|---|
| oxygen | ☐ |
| magnesium | ☑ |
| carbon | ☐ |
| nitrogen | ☐ |

This gets 0 mark. →

Which of these elements is a metal?

Tick the correct box.

| | |
|---|---|
| oxygen | ☐ |
| magnesium | ☑ |
| carbon | ☑ |
| nitrogen | ☐ |

■ Complete a sentence by choosing a word from the list.

You *must* use a word from the list.

So *nitrogen* is incorrect because, although it is a gas at room temperature, it is not in the list.

Complete the sentence by choosing a word from the list.

**iron     zinc     sulphur     oxygen**

Of these elements, the one that is a gas at room temperature is _oxygen_ .

■ From the information in the chart, choose the best answer to the question.

The example opposite uses a bar chart. You have to get both metals right to get the mark.

Other metals such as iron and nickel have higher melting points, but are incorrect because they are not in the chart.

From the information in the chart, choose the **two** metals with the highest melting points.

_gold and copper_

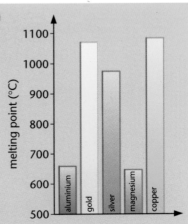

172

■ In some questions you will need to give short answers of one word, a few words or one sentence.

    Clues: there will only be one line for your answer.

        there will only be one mark for a correct answer (shown in the margin).

There's no need to write any more (e.g. *using a Bunsen burner*). There's only 1 mark, so it's a waste of time.

> How can crystals of magnesium sulphate be formed from a dilute solution of magnesium sulphate.
>
> *Heat it gently.*            1 mark
>
> or
>
> How can crystals of magnesium sulphate be formed from a dilute solution of magnesium sulphate.
>
> *Let the water evaporate.*      1 mark

---

■ In other questions you will need to give longer answers.

    Clues: there will be two or more lines for your answer.

        there will be two or more marks for a correct answer.

These questions will often ask you to 'describe' or 'explain'. Make sure you know the difference between these two instructions.

this describes →

this explains →

> The new iron railings around a school field soon begin to rust.
>
> Describe **two** suitable ways that could be used to prevent rusting.
>
> Explain how these methods work.
>
> *The railings could be painted or they could be galvanised (coated in zinc).*
>
> *These methods work because they both prevent oxygen and water from reaching the iron and reacting with it.*

---

■ Often in a question you will see a word or words in **bold** type. This usually emphasises what you need to give in your answer.

To give more examples is time wasted.

> Give **one** example of an igneous rock.
>
> *granite*            1 mark

> The diagram shows the particles in a solid.
>
>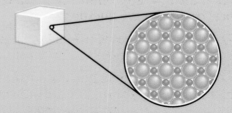
>
> **In terms of particles**, explain why it is difficult to squash a solid.
>
> *The particles are held close together by strong bonds and are in fixed positions.*

Your answer must give an explanation 'in terms of particles', so an answer *'because solids are hard and keep their shape'* is incorrect.

■ When asked to 'calculate' an answer, you may be told to show your working. This is important because you may gain some of the marks even if your final answer is wrong.

(a) Units may be provided.
    If they are provided do *not* change them.

Calculate the volume of the block of copper, in cm³. Show your working.

$volume = length \times breadth \times height$

$= 3\,cm \times 2\,cm \times 2\,cm$

$= 12\,cm^3$

2 cm    2 cm
← 3 cm →

(b) You may be asked to write in the units.

The volume of a piece of calcium is 6 cm³ and its mass is 9 g.
Calculate the density of calcium.
Show your working. Give the units.

You may not get any marks without the units.

$density = \dfrac{mass}{volume} = \dfrac{9\,g}{6\,cm^3} = 1.5\,g/cm^3$

---

■ When you are asked to complete a diagram, you must do so neatly and accurately and exactly as instructed.

Use a ruler for lines that should be straight.

The diagram opposite has been completed but has several errors.
How many mistakes can you spot?

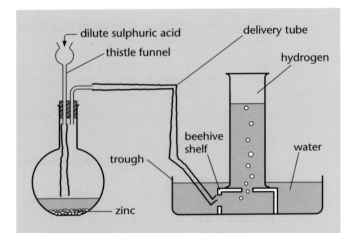

Complete the diagram to show how you would make and collect some hydrogen.

This is a correct completion.

Lines should be drawn with a ruler.

The tube from the thistle funnel should extend below the surface of the liquid.

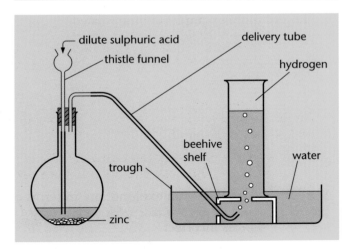

■ In some questions you have to draw lines for labels or to join boxes.

■ When you are asked to label a diagram, draw the guide lines accurately and precisely.

The line to the core is well drawn. The line to the crust is *not* well drawn. It could be pointing to the magma (molten rock).

On the diagram which shows the structure of the Earth
draw a line from letter E to the core,
draw a line from the letter F to the crust.

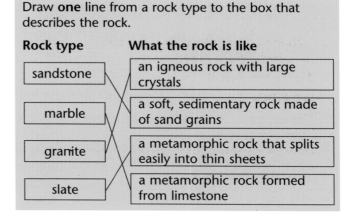

■ Joining boxes: read *all* the statements before you begin. Link together pairs of boxes only with clear lines.

Draw **one** line from a rock type to the box that describes the rock.

| Rock type | What the rock is like |
|---|---|
| sandstone | an igneous rock with large crystals |
| marble | a soft, sedimentary rock made of sand grains |
| granite | a metamorphic rock that splits easily into thin sheets |
| slate | a metamorphic rock formed from limestone |

■ In all your answers, try to be as precise as possible. You won't get any marks for vague answers.

For example 'it has used up all the air' is too vague and you will get 0 marks.

Don't write down two different answers when you're not sure. That way you are bound to get no marks.

So 0 mark.

Choose the answer you think is most likely to be correct.

This experiment shows a candle burning then going out.

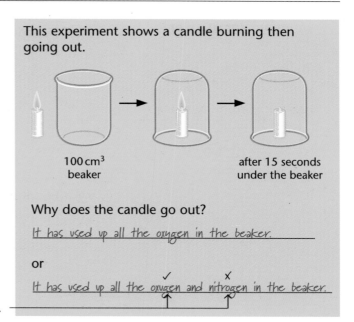

100 cm³
beaker

after 15 seconds
under the beaker

Why does the candle go out?

It has used up all the oxygen in the beaker.

or

It has used up all the oxygen and nitrogen in the beaker.   ✓   ✗

■ Some questions are about graphs.

Line graphs often have both axes with scales and are labelled. Look at these carefully before attempting an answer.
Accurate readings from the graph are necessary. A ruler may help.

You must also take care to be accurate if you are asked to plot points on the graph.

Look carefully at the scale. There is 0 mark for 59 or 61 grams.

You may be asked what the shape of the graph tells you (the trend).

The solubility of a substance is the number of grams that will dissolve in 100 grams of water.
The graph shows how the solubility of potassium nitrate varies between 0°C and 60°C.

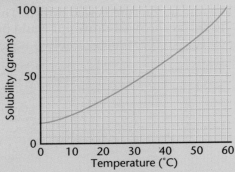

(a) How much potassium nitrate dissolves in 100 grams of water at 40°C?

_60 grams_

(b) How does the temperature affect the solubility of potassium nitrate?

_Increasing the temperature increases the solubility._

---

■ Do not be surprised to be asked about experiments you have not done or seen demonstrated.

Use your knowledge and understanding of scientific methods and apply these to new or unfamiliar situations.

Chris knows that water boils at 100°C. He noticed that water with salt dissolved in it boiled at a slightly higher temperature. He did an experiment to see if there was a link between the amount of salt dissolved and the boiling point.

Chris measured out 100 cm³ of water and poured it into a beaker. He added 1 gram of salt and stirred slowly until it dissolved. He heated the mixture and recorded the boiling point. He repeated the experiment five times, each time using an extra gram of salt.

(a) Why is it important to use 100 g of water in each test?

_for a fair test_

(b) Which piece of apparatus could he use to measure out 100 cm³ of water?

_a measuring cylinder_

(c) How could he measure the boiling point of water?

_use a thermometer_

(d) He found it took quite a long time to dissolve 6 grams of salt in the 100 cm³ of water. How could he get it to dissolve more quickly?

_Stir the mixture faster._

**Remember that if you have some time left, go back to try any difficult parts of questions that you left and to check your answers for careless mistakes.**

# 'What you need to remember' completed passages

## EVERYDAY MATERIALS

### 1.1 The right one for the job

The things that make a material good for a particular job, like how hard it is, are called its **properties**.

Materials you can see through are **transparent**.

All metals let electricity pass through them. They are called **conductors**.
Materials that do not let electricity through are called **insulators**.

### 1.2 Solid, liquid and gas

Solids have their own **shape**. Liquids and gases can **change** shape. A gas spreads out to fill any **space**.

Gases and liquids will **flow** through pipes.

Solids and liquids are heavier substances than gases; we say they are **denser**.

Something floats on a liquid if it is **less dense** than the liquid.
A lump of iron **sinks** in water because it is a denser substance than water.

### 1.3 Explaining the way things are

Solids, liquids and gases are all made of **particles**.

In solids, the particles hold each other together **strongly**. They cannot change places, but they can **vibrate**.

In liquids, the particles stay close together but they can **change places** with each other. This means you can **pour** a liquid.

In a gas there is a lot of space between the particles. The particles **move** around at high speed.

You can squash a gas because the particles are **far apart**. It is hard to squash a liquid or a solid because the particles are **close together**.

### 1.4 Mixing solids and liquids

When a substance dissolves in a liquid we get a **solution**.

Substances often dissolve better when the liquid is **hot**.

The liquid that the substance goes into is called the **solvent**. The dissolved substance is called the **solute**.

### 1.5 Melting and boiling

Many solids have a temperature at which they will melt. This is called the **melting point** of the solid.

The temperature at which a liquid boils is called the **boiling point**. As a liquid boils, it changes into a **gas**.

Boiling point temperatures are always **higher** than melting point temperatures.

### 1.6 Heat in, heat out

When we boil a liquid, we give **energy** to the liquid.

When an ice cube is melted we **transfer** heat to the ice.

The change from liquid to gas is called **evaporation**.

We can make evaporation happen more quickly by **heating** the liquid, and by **blowing** on the liquid surface.

Evaporation makes things get **colder**.

### 1.7 Other effects of heating and cooling

If a solid or liquid or gas is heated, it will **expand**.

If we cool the solid or liquid or gas down, then it will **contract**.

Expanding materials produce **push** forces. Contracting materials produce **pull** forces. These forces can be very large and cause lots of damage.

### 1.8 Looking at change

When things change, the **mass** doesn't change.

Changes which don't produce new substances are called **physical** changes.

Physical changes are usually easy to **reverse**.

## CHEMICAL SUBSTANCES

### 2.1 Mixtures

Air and sea-water are both **mixtures**.

Air is a mixture of gases. The two main gases in the air are **nitrogen** and **oxygen**.

The sea is a mixture of water, **salt** and lots of other things.

Mixtures can be **split** up into their different parts. For example, you can get the salt out of sea-water by **evaporating** the water.

You can change the **amounts** of different things in a mixture.

## 2.2 Taking out the bits

Filter paper acts like a very fine **sieve**.

We can **separate** a mixture of liquid and particles of solid using filter paper. We call this **filtering**.

The **solid** left behind in the filter paper is called the residue.
The liquid that goes through the filter paper is called the **filtrate**.

## 2.3 Getting the liquid back

When a solid dissolves in water we can get the water back by **distillation**.

This works because the water **boils** and turns into steam.

The steam is cooled to **condense** it.

The **solids** get left behind.

The water we get at the end is pure. It is called **distilled** water.

## 2.4 What's in a colour?

Chromatography is used to split up a mixture of substances that **dissolve** in the same liquid.

The substances spread out through the paper at different **speeds**.

The pattern you get is called a **chromatogram**.

## 2.5 Elements

An element is a substance that cannot be split into anything **simpler**.

Water is made from the two elements **hydrogen** and **oxygen**.

Altogether there are about 90 **elements** that make up everything else.

## 2.6 Shorthand for elements

Every element has **a symbol**. This is either one or two letters.

The first letter is always a **capital** letter.

## 2.7 Putting elements together

A substance which contains two or more elements joined together (combined) is called a **compound**.

Compounds have different **properties** from the elements they contain.

Many compounds are formed by **chemical** reactions between elements.

## 2.8 Useful compounds

The best-known liquid in the world is **water**.

A solid compound used to make lots of other substances is **salt**.

Air contains small amounts of **carbon** dioxide gas.

Water, salt and carbon dioxide are all very important **compounds**.

# METALS AND NON-METALS

## 3.1 Looking at metals

Metals are normally shiny and **hard**.

Metals conduct **electricity**.

Metals **conduct** heat.

Iron and steel are **magnetic**.

## 3.2 Non-metals

Elements that are not metals are called **non-metals**.

Non-metals can be solids, liquids or **gases**.

If we know an element is a **gas**, then we also know that it is a non-metal.

Most non-metals do not **conduct** heat or electricity.

Solid non-metals are **brittle**.

## 3.3 Where do we find non-metals?

Most of the things around us are made from **non-metals**.

Life is based on a non-metal called **carbon**.

We need to breathe a non-metal called **oxygen**.

Oxygen is also needed for **burning**.

## 3.4 Elements of Thar

An element is a metal or a **non-metal**.

Any element that is a **gas** must be a non-metal.

We can test to see if an element is a metal or a non-metal. Metals conduct **heat** and **electricity**. Most non-metals do not conduct.

## 3.5 Metals reacting with oxygen

A few metals burn very easily in the air's **oxygen**.

Metals that burn brightest are the most **reactive**.

## 3.6 Metals reacting with water

Some metals, for example magnesium:
- react slowly with **water**;
- react more quickly with **steam**.

A few metals react quickly with water, for example **sodium**.

All these reactions make a gas called **hydrogen**.

Some metals do not react with water, for example **copper**.

## 3.7 Which metals push hardest?

A reactive metal has a bigger **push** than a less reactive metal.

A reactive metal **displaces** a less reactive metal. We call this a **displacement** reaction.

## 3.8 Which metals react best?

We can list metals in order of **reactivity**. This list is called the **reactivity series**.

We put the most reactive at the **top** of the list, and the least reactive at the **bottom**.

The reactivity series is useful for **predicting** how a metal will react.

## CHEMICAL REACTIONS

## 4.1 Chemical changes

Chemical changes always make **new** substances.

Life itself involves **chemical** changes.

## 4.2 Acids

Acids are substances that taste **sour**.

Some acids, like sulphuric acid, are dangerous because they are **corrosive**.

## 4.3 How can we tell whether something is an acid?

Indicators are special **dyes**. They change **colour** when mixed with acids or alkalis.

Universal indicator helps us to measure a substance's **pH**.

Alkalis have a pH of **more** than 7.
Acids have a pH of **less** than 7.
Neutral substances have a pH **equal** to 7.

## 4.4 Getting rid of an acid with an alkali

When we mix an alkali with an acid, we get a reaction called **neutralisation**.

Neutralisation reactions make two new substances, a **salt** and **water**.

To help us know when neutralisation is complete, we use an **indicator**.

## 4.5 Using neutralisation reactions

We can neutralise an acid with an **alkali**.

We can also neutralise acids by using sodium bicarbonate or a **carbonate**. These react with the acid to give the gas **carbon dioxide**.

## 4.6 How do metals react with acids?

Metals react with dilute acids to make a **salt**.

Metals push **hydrogen** out of the acid.

## 4.7 Salt and salts

We know sodium chloride as common **salt**.

There are **hundreds** of different salts.

A salt usually contains a metal element joined to at least one **non-metal**.

Salts form **crystals**.

Most salts dissolve in **water**.

## 4.8 Other kinds of chemical reaction

A chemical reaction that joins oxygen to a substance is called **oxidation**.

Examples of oxidation are rusting, respiration and **combustion**.

If we heat a substance and it breaks down, we call this thermal **decomposition**.

## 4.9 Writing down chemical reactions

Chemical reactions make **new** substances.

We show what happens in chemical reactions by writing word **equations**.

We put what we start with on the **left**.

We put what we finish with on the **right**.

# EARTH CHEMISTRY

## 5.1 Different types of rock

Carbon dioxide gas is produced when acid is put on **calcium carbonate**.

Hot liquid rock deep in the Earth is called **magma**.

Rocks made from magma are called **igneous** rocks. Examples of igneous rocks are **basalt** and **granite**.

## 5.2 Getting new rocks from old

New rocks made under the sea from the bits that wear off the old rocks are called **sedimentary** rocks. These rocks are formed over **millions** of years.

Rocks can also be made from other rocks by **heat** and **pressure**. For example, heat changes limestone into **marble**, and pressure changes mudstone into **slate**.

Because marble and slate are both made by changing other rocks, we call them **metamorphic** rocks.

## 5.3 The rock cycle

The substances that make up rocks shift around over **millions** of years.
We call this shift the **rock cycle**.

## 5.4 How the weather breaks up rocks

When rocks are worn away by the weather, we call it **weathering**.

Changes in temperature from hot to cold can make **cracks** in the surface of a rock. Water gets in cracks and makes them bigger. This happens because water **expands** when it freezes.

Sometimes freezing water makes bits of rock **break** off.

Rocks and building materials are also worn away by bits blown in the **wind**. This is called **erosion**.

## 5.5 Acids in the air

Air contains **carbon dioxide**. This gas dissolves in rain water to make a very weak **acid**. This attacks building stone such as **limestone**. We call this process **chemical** weathering.

When we burn fuels we also make gases such as sulphur **dioxide** and nitrogen **oxides**. These are much more acidic and cause chemical weathering much **faster**.

## 5.6 Things we can do with limestone

Chemical **reactions** are used to make useful materials.

If you heat limestone, you make it into a useful substance called **calcium oxide**. The other name for calcium oxide is **quicklime**.

If you add water to quicklime, you get another useful substance called **slaked** lime. The other name for slaked lime is **calcium hydroxide**.

Lime water is made by dissolving calcium hydroxide in water. Lime water turns milky when **carbon dioxide** is bubbled through it.

## 5.7 Getting metals from rocks

You can find some metals such as gold, silver and copper as lumps in the ground. These are called **native** metals.

Most metals come from rocks called **ores**.

Iron ore contains oxygen joined with **iron**.

We get the iron from the ore by taking away the **oxygen**. This is done by heating it in a **blast** furnace.

We have to use electricity to extract **aluminium** from aluminium oxide. This process is called **electrolysis**.

## 5.8 A problem with metals

Rusting is a chemical **reaction**.

Iron only rusts when in both air and water **together**.

Metals such as **bronze** do not rust. But they do **corrode**.

Polluted air causes much faster corrosion of **metals**.

## 5.9 Why do we keep on polluting the air?

Something that we can burn easily and safely is called a **fuel**. When fuels burn, they release **energy**.

Car engines make harmful gases called **nitrogen oxides**.

Power stations produce some sulphur **dioxide**. This makes **acid rain**.

# MATTER

## C1.1 Using everyday materials

We make things from **materials**.

We use different materials to do different **jobs**. This is because they have different **properties**.

## C1.2 Metals and non-metals

Most of the elements are **metals**.

All metals are good conductors of heat and **electricity**, but most non-metals do not **conduct** heat or electricity.

Elements which are gases at room temperature are all **non-metals**.

## C1.3 Solids, liquids and gases

A solid has its own shape and **volume**.

A liquid has its own volume but not its own **shape**.

A gas does not have either its own shape or its own volume. It spreads out to fill all the **space** it can.

A gas can be **compressed**.

Liquids and gases can **flow**.

## C1.4 Making models of matter

Solids have their own **shape** because the particles cannot move around. Liquids and gases flow because their particles can **move** around each other.

You cannot compress liquids and solids easily because there is no space between their **particles**. You can compress a gas because there is **space** between the particles.

## C1.5 Getting warmer, getting colder

When we heat solids, liquids or gases, they normally **expand**.

When solids, liquids and gases cool down, they normally **contract**.

If we stop a gas expanding when it gets hot, we get an increase in **pressure**.

## C1.6 Mixtures

You can mix things together in different amounts. We say that they can be mixed in different **proportions**.

When you dissolve a solid in a liquid, the **particles** of the solid and the liquid get mixed together.

Air is a **mixture** of gases.

## C1.7 Making pure white sugar

We get sugar from plants such as sugar cane. The sugar is **mixed** up with many other things. To get pure white sugar, we need to **separate** it from these other things. We can do this because sugar **dissolves** in water. We say that it is **soluble** in water.

We can make more sugar dissolve by using **more** water, or **hotter** water.

## C1.8 Separating mixtures

Most substances in the world around us are parts of **mixtures**.

A substance that is not mixed up with other substances is called a **pure** substance.

To get a pure substance, we need to **separate** it from other substances. We can do this because different substances have different **properties**.

## C1.9 What is density?                    C+

A piece of steel weighs more than the same **volume** of water. So we say that steel is **denser** than water.

The density of a material is its **mass** divided by its volume.

## C1.10 Density of gases                    C+

When you **squeeze** a gas, the particles move **closer** together. This increases the **density** of the gas.

## C1.11 What makes a solid melt?            C+

When you heat up a solid, you make its particles vibrate **faster**.

The particles start to move around if they **vibrate** strongly enough. The solid has changed into a **liquid**. It has **melted**.

## C1.12 Why do liquids evaporate?           C+

When a liquid changes into a gas, we say that it **evaporates**.

A liquid evaporates as faster moving particles **escape**.

Heating speeds up evaporation because more particles have enough **energy** to escape.

## C1.13 Melting, boiling and temperature C+

When a solid is melting or a liquid is boiling, its **temperature** doesn't change.

The energy transferred to a melting solid makes the particles **break away** from their fixed positions.

The energy transferred to a boiling liquid makes its particles **escape**.

## C1.14 How does a gas fill its container?  C+

The particles of a gas move about with rapid, **random** motion. So a gas spreads out into all the space it can. We say that the gas **diffuses**.

## C1.15 How can you change gas pressure?C+

You can increase the pressure of a gas:

- by squeezing it into a smaller **space**;
- by increasing its **temperature**, which makes the particles hit the sides of the container **harder**.

Both squeezing and heating the gas make its particles hit the sides of the container more **often**.

## C1.16 Why do solids expand when they are heated?                               C+

The particles in a solid are held in position by strong **forces** of attraction. The particles can't move about but they can **vibrate**.

When a solid is heated, the vibrating particles bang into each other and take up more space, so the solid **expands**.

## MORE CHEMICAL REACTIONS

## C2.1 Two sorts of change

We call changes that make new substances **chemical** changes. Changes that do not make new substances are **physical** changes.

Two examples of physical change are changes of **state**, and separating **mixtures**.

Physical changes are usually easier to **reverse** than chemical changes.

Chemical changes are produced by chemical **reactions**.

## C2.2 Chemical reactions

Another name for burning is combustion. When things burn they react with **oxygen**. So we also call burning an **oxidation** reaction.

In a thermal decomposition reaction, you split up a substance by **heating** it.

In electrolysis, you split up a substance by passing an **electric current** through it.

## C2.3 Elements and atoms

We call simple substances **elements**.

Elements are made up of very small particles called **atoms**.

All the atoms in one element are the **same** kind.

Atoms of different elements are **different**.

## C2.4 Compounds

Substances made from atoms of different elements joined together are called **compounds**.

A substance made from different atoms <u>not</u> joined together is called a **mixture**.

Compounds have different **properties** from the elements they are made from.

## C2.5 Elements reacting with oxygen

When we burn elements in oxygen, we get compounds called **oxides**.
We say that these are **oxidation** reactions.

Some non-metallic elements make oxides that dissolve in water to make **acids**.

Some metals make oxides that dissolve in water to make **alkalis**.

## C2.6 Metals reacting with acids

Most metals react with dilute **acids**. The reactions produce a gas called **hydrogen**. They also produce compounds called **salts**.

We can write down the reaction between zinc and hydrochloric acid like this:

**zinc** + dilute hydrochloric acid → zinc **chloride** + hydrogen

## C2.7 Displacement reactions

Some metals are more **reactive** than others.

A reactive metal will push a less reactive metal out of a **solution** of one of its compounds. We call this type of chemical change a **displacement** reaction.

A list of metals in order of their reactivities is called a **reactivity series**.

## C2.8 Carrying out tests

When we want to find out what a substance is, we carry out chemical **tests**. Most tests are **chemical** changes.

*You need to know what each of these tests tells you.*

## C2.9 Physical change and mass  C+

In a physical change you still have the same substances made from the same **particles**. So in a physical change there is no change in **mass**.

## C2.10 Chemical change and mass  C+

In chemical reactions, there is no change in **mass**. This is because there are still the same **atoms**. They are just joined together in **different** ways.

## C2.11 Different kinds of mixtures  C+

We can have a **mixture** of elements, or of **compounds**. We can also **mix** elements and compounds together.

## C2.12 More about compounds and mixtures  C+

In a mixture, elements can be mixed together in different **ratios**.

But in a compound, the atoms of the different elements are always joined together in the **same** ratio. We say that compounds have a fixed **composition**.

## C2.13 Simple chemical formulas  C+

*You should be able to use the formula of a compound to tell you what elements are in the compound and the ratio of their atoms.*

## C2.14 More about chemical formulas  C+

The atoms of some elements go round in pairs called **molecules**.

## C2.15 More complicated chemical formulas  C+

*You need to be able to work out which elements are in the compound (and what numbers of atoms they have) just as you have for the compounds on this page.*

## C2.16 Energy changes in chemical reactions  C+

When the atoms of two elements join together, the reaction usually gives out **energy**.

Reactions which **split** up compounds take energy in.

## C2.17 More about the reactivity series  C+

When a metal reacts with water, the products are a gas called **hydrogen** and a metal compound called a **hydroxide**.

## C2.18 Adding non-metals to the reactivity series  C+

We can include hydrogen and **carbon** in the reactivity series for the metals even though they are **non-metals**.

# EARTH SCIENCE

## C3.1 Different kinds of rocks

When molten rock cools down **igneous** rocks are formed.

**Sedimentary** rocks form at the bottom of lakes and seas. They are made up of sediment that builds up in **layers**.

Heat and pressure can change rocks. We call the new rocks **metamorphic** rocks.

## C3.2 Heating up the rock cycle

We live on the Earth's **crust**.

As we go deeper into the Earths crust, it gets very **hot**.

Between the crust and the core, there is a layer of molten rock (magma) called the **mantle**.

Rocks slowly move around all the time. We call this the **rock cycle**. The energy for this movement comes from **radioactive** substances and from the **weather**.

## C3.3 Getting metals out of rocks

A metal found in the ground as itself is said to be **native**.
Rocks that contain metals or metal compounds are called **ores**.

When we use a chemical reaction to get a metal out of its ore, we call this **smelting**.
We smelt iron in a **blast furnace**.

More reactive metals cannot be got from their ores by heating with **carbon** so they are smelted using **electricity**.

## C3.4 Corroding metals

Rusting is a special case of **corrosion**. Rusting takes place when iron or steel is in contact with both air and **water**.

Most methods of slowing down rusting use a **barrier**. One of the best barriers is **zinc**.

The less reactive a metal is, the less likely it is to **corrode**.

## C3.5 Acids and alkalis

Sulphur dioxide from volcanoes and nitrogen oxides from lightning are **acidic** gases.

The opposites of acids are **alkalis**.

Chemists tell the difference between acids and alkalis by using **indicators**. These are often natural **dyes**. In acids and alkalis, they change **colour**.

## C3.6 Acids in the soil

We use universal indicator to measure **pH**.

A pH of 7 means that the solution is **neutral**. When the pH is less than 7, we have an **acidic** solution. When the pH is more than 7, we have an **alkaline** solution.

When an alkali neutralises an acid, we get a **salt** and **water** only.

When a carbonate neutralises an acid, we get a salt, water and **carbon dioxide**.

## C3.7 Weathering rocks

Rocks are broken down into smaller pieces by the Sun, the **wind**, water and **ice**. This is called **physical weathering**.

Chemical reactions can also attack rocks; we call this **chemical** weathering.

## C3.8 Looking after the environment     C+

Fossil fuels contain carbon and **hydrogen**. When fossil fuels or fuels made from fossil fuels burn, they produce carbon dioxide and **water**.

The useful thing that we get from fossil fuels is **energy**.

The motor car also produces small amounts of carbon monoxide and **nitrogen oxides**.

## C3.9 More about the rock cycle     C+

When plates in the Earth's crust collide, rocks are slowly pushed up to form **mountains**.

The rocks at the top of the new mountain can be igneous, metamorphic or **sedimentary**. These rocks are then broken down by **weathering** and **erosion**.

They are carried down the mountainside; this is called **transportation**.

When bits of rock reach a lake or the sea they form a sediment; this is called **deposition**. Later, new rock is formed as the sediment gets covered up; this is called **burial**.

## C3.10 Smelting metals     C+

The more **reactive** the metal, the more **energy** is needed to extract it.

We smelt metals in the middle of the reactivity series, like iron, with **carbon**. But for metals higher in the reactivity series, like aluminium, we use **electricity**.

## C3.11 More about salts     C+

Hydrochloric acid makes salts called **chlorides**. Sulphuric acid makes salts called **sulphates**. Nitric acid makes salts called **nitrates**.

## C3.12 Why are ice and water so strange? C+

When water freezes, it **expands**. This means that the molecules in ice are **further away** from each other than the molecules in water. This is why ice is less **dense** than water.

## C3.13 Why do some rocks dissolve?     C+

Carbon dioxide dissolves in water to make a very weak **acid**. This reacts with calcium carbonate rocks to make a soluble substance called **calcium bicarbonate**. So the rock slowly **dissolves**.

## C3.14 Carbon dioxide and the greenhouse effect     C+

One of the greenhouse gases is **carbon dioxide**.

The amount of carbon dioxide in the air increases because we burn **fossil fuels**.

An increase in the greenhouse effect will raise the Earth's average **temperature**.

## C3.15 Waste and pollution     C+

Waste is a problem because it can never just **disappear**.

To prevent pollution, we must change waste into **harmless** substances.

# Glossary/index

A few words that occur very often such as force, energy, animal, plant, electricity, chemical and reaction are not included. Some of these words are part of the headings of the nine topics in the book. Words in *italics* appear elsewhere in the glossary.

## A

**acid rain:** rain that is *acidic* because it has *sulphur dioxide* and/or *nitrogen dioxides* dissolved in it   67, 93

**acids:** *solutions* that react with many metals to produce a *salt* and *hydrogen*, and that react with *alkalis* to produce a *salt* and *water*   58, 60–69, 84–85, 126, 128–129, 152–155

**air:** a *mixture* of *gases*, mainly *nitrogen* and *oxygen*, that surrounds us   26, 47, 105, 108

**air pollution:** harmful *gases* such as *sulphur dioxide* or *nitrogen dioxides* in the *air*   84–85, 92–93

**alkalis:** the opposite of *acids*; they react with *acids* to produce *salts*   62–67, 126, 152–155

**aluminium:** a *metal* that you get from its *ore*, bauxite, using electricity   89

**atom:** the smallest *particle* of an *element*   123–125, 137

## B

**blast furnace:** used for *smelting iron ore*   149

**boiling point:** the temperature at which a *liquid* boils   18–19, 114

**bonds:** the forces that hold *atoms* together in a *molecule*   124, 141

**burning:** when substances react with *oxygen* and release *thermal energy*; also called *combustion*   39, 58, 72, 120

## C

**calcium:** a *metal element*   76, 86

**calcium carbonate:** the chemical *compound* that *limestone* and *marble* are made from   76, 86

**calcium hydroxide:** the substance made when *calcium oxide* reacts with *water*; it dissolves slightly in water to make *lime-water*   2, 87

**calcium oxide:** a substance made by *thermal decomposition* of *limestone*   86

**carbon:** a *solid non-metal element*   41, 97, 127, 162

**carbonates:** *compounds* that react with *acids* to produce *carbon dioxide*   67, 76, 155

**carbon dioxide:** 1. a *gas* whose *molecules* are made from *carbon atoms* and *oxygen atoms*   42, 120, 155, 165–166

2. test for carbon dioxide   87, 121, 132

**carbon monoxide:** a poisonous *gas* produced in small quantities when a car burns petrol or diesel   159

**cement:** the material that holds the grains together in a *sedimentary* rock   145

**chemical change:** a change that produces new substances   39, 58–59, 118–121, 135

**chlorine:** 1. a *non-metal element*; it is a poisonous, greeny-yellow *gas*   38, 56, 121, 133

2. test for chlorine   121, 133

**chromatogram:** the separated substances, usually on paper, that you get by using *chromatography*   32–33

**chromatography:** a way of separating different *dissolved solids*, for example dyes   32–33, 108

**combine:** join together; *atoms* of different *elements* combine to make new substances   135–136

**combustion:** another word for *burning*   120

**compress; compression:** to squeeze into a smaller space   99, 101

**compound:** a substance made from the *atoms* of two, or more, different *elements* joined together   38–41, 75, 124–125, 137–138

**condense, condensation:** changing a *gas* to a *liquid* by cooling it   25, 30–31

**conductor: 1. electrical** a substance that an electrical current easily passes through   11, 42, 96

**2. thermal** a substance that *thermal energy* easily passes through   42

**contract, contraction:** *solids, liquids* and *gases* do this when they cool   22–23, 102–103

**copper:** a *metal element* which is not very reactive   51–53

**corrosion:** what happens to *metals* when they react with chemicals such as *water, oxygen* or *acids* in the *air*   150–151

# D

**decomposition:** splitting up a *compound* into simpler substances   73, 121

**dense:** a dense substance has a lot of *mass* in a small *volume*   13, 110–111

**density:** the *mass* of a certain *volume*, e.g. 1 cm$^3$, of a substance   110–111

**diffuse, diffusion:** the spreading out of a *gas* because its *particles* are moving about   115

**displace, displacement:** when a more reactive *element* pushes a less reactive element out of one of its *compounds*   54–55, 130–131

**dissolve:** when the *particles* of a *solid* completely mix with the particles of a *liquid* to make a clear *solution*   16–17, 58, 105–107, 119, 165

**distil, distillation:** evaporating a *liquid* and then *condensing* it again to get a pure *liquid*   25, 31, 107, 109

# E

**element:** a substance that can't be split up into anything simpler   34–39, 44–49, 96–97, 102–103

**erosion:** the process where *wind, water* and *ice*, break down rocks into smaller pieces then carry them away   83, 161

**evaporate, evaporation:** when a *liquid* changes into a *gas*   21, 27, 30–31, 113

**expand, expansion:** when things get bigger, usually because they are hotter   22–23, 82, 102–103, 117

# F

**filter, filtering:** separating a *liquid* from an undissolved *solid* by passing it through small holes, usually in paper; the solid doesn't pass through the holes and is left behind   28–29, 107

**filtrate:** the *liquid* that passes through a *filter*   28

**formula:** uses *symbols* to tell you how many *atoms* of each *element* are joined together to form a *compound* (or *molecule* of an *element*)   138–140

**fossil fuels:** fuels that were formed from the remains of animals or plants that died millions of years ago; they are burned to release *thermal energy*   158–159

# G

**gases:** substances that spread out (*diffuse*) to fill all the space they can; they can be squeezed (*compressed*) into a smaller *volume*   2, 14–15, 99–101, 103, 109–111, 113, 115

**geothermal energy:** energy stored in hot rocks in the Earth's crust   146

**granite:** a type of *igneous* rock with large *crystals*:   76–76, 144

**greenhouse effect:** *gases*, such as *carbon dioxide*, in the *air* that make the Earth warmer than it would otherwise be   166

# H

**hydrogen:** 1. a *non-metal element*; it is a *gas* that burns to make *water*    **35, 53, 68–69, 129, 131–132, 142**

2. test for hydrogen    **129, 132**

# I

**igneous:** rocks that are formed when molten *magma* from inside the Earth cools down    **133, 153–155**

**indicator:** a substance that can change colour and tell you if a solution is an *acid* or an *alkali*    **62–63, 144–146**

**insoluble:** how we describe a substance that will not *dissolve*    **106–107**

**insulator:** a substance that will not let an electric current pass through it    **11**

**iron:** a *metal element* that is attracted by a magnet; steel is made mainly from iron    **42–43, 50–51, 89**

# L

**limestone:** a *sedimentary* rock made from *calcium carbonate*    **76, 84–87**

**lime-water:** a clear *solution* of *calcium hydroxide* in water; it is turned cloudy by *carbon dioxide*    **87, 121, 132**

**liquid:** substances that have a fixed *volume* but take the shape of their container    **12, 14–15, 98–99, 103, 112–113**

**litmus:** an *indicator* that is red in *acids* and blue in *alkalis*    **126–127, 133**

# M

**magma:** molten rock beneath the Earth's crust    **146**

**magnesium:** a reactive *metal element* that burns brightly    **39, 51–52, 58, 68**

**mantle:** a layer of material in the Earth, between the crust and the core, made up mainly of molten rock (*magma*)    **147**

**marble:** a *metamorphic* rock made from *limestone*    **76, 79**

**mass:** the amount of stuff in an object; it is measured in grams (g) or kilograms (kg)    **24, 134–135**

**melt:** changing a *solid* into a *liquid* by heating it    **18, 20, 112, 114**

**melting point:** the temperature at which a solid *melts*    **18**

**mercury:** the only *metal element* that is a *liquid* at ordinary room temperature    **42**

**metals:** substances that conduct electricity; they are usually shiny and often hard    **42–43, 50–56, 68–69, 96–97, 126, 128–131, 142, 148–151, 162**

**metamorphic:** rocks that are made when other rocks are changed (but not melted) by heat and pressure    **79, 144–146**

**mixture:** different substances that are mixed but not joined together    **26–27, 104, 109, 124, 136–137**

**molecule:** the smallest part of a chemical *compound*    **105, 137**

# N

**native metals:** these are found in the Earth's crust as the *metals* themselves rather than as *compounds*    **88, 148**

**neutral:** what we call a *solution* that is neither *acid* nor *alkali*    **62–63, 153**

**neutralisation:** a reaction between an *acid* and an *alkali* that produced a *neutral solution* of a *salt* (plus more *water*)    **64–67, 154–155**

**nitrogen:** the main *gas* in *air*; it is fairly unreactive but will react with the *oxygen* in the *air* at high temperatures    **26, 47, 105**

**nitrogen oxides:** *acidic gases* produced when *nitrogen* reacts with *oxygen* at high temperatures   **85, 92, 152, 157, 159**

**non-metals:** what we call *elements* that aren't *metals*   **44–47, 96–97, 126**

# O

**ores:** *compounds* of *metal* and *non-metal elements* that are found in the Earth's crust   **88–89, 148–149**

**oxidation:** *oxygen* joining with other *elements* to make compounds called *oxides*; for example, *burning* and *rusting*   **72–73, 120, 126–127**

**oxide:** *compounds* of *oxygen* and other *elements*   **39, 50–51, 126**

**oxygen: 1.** one of the two main *gases* in air; it is needed for things to *burn*   **26, 47, 50–51, 72–73, 120, 126–127**

**2.** test for oxygen   **122, 131**

# P

**particles:** the very small bits that everything is made of   **14–15, 100–101, 105, 110–111, 115–118, 164**

**pH:** a scale of numbers that tells you how strong an *acid* or *alkali* is   **63, 154**

**physical change:** a change such as *melting* or *dissolving* that doesn't produce new substances; it is usually easy to reverse   **24–25, 118–119, 134**

**pollute:** contaminate the environment with undesirable materials or energy   **158–159, 167**

**pollution:** harmful chemicals that humans allow into the *air*, soil or *water* around them (the environment)   **158–159, 167**

**potassium:** a *metal element* that has properties and *compounds* similar to those of *sodium*   **62, 65**

**pressure:** how much force there is on a certain area   **63, 111, 116**

**products:** the new substances made in a *chemical reaction*   **135**

**properties:** what a material is like, for example whether it conducts electricity or whether it burns   **10–13, 94–95, 109, 125**

# R

**reactants:** the substances we start with in a *chemical reaction*   **135**

**reactivity series:** a list of *metals* in order of how quickly they react with *oxygen, water* or *acids*   **56–57, 128–131, 142–143, 148–149, 162**

**recycle:** to use materials over and over again   **167**

**reduction:** to remove *oxygen* from a *compound* in a *chemical reaction*   **162**

**residue:** the bits of *solid* that are trapped by a *filter*   **28**

**respire, respiration:** the breakdown of food, using *oxygen*, to release energy in living cells; *carbon dioxide* and *water* are waste products   **72**

**rock cycle:** the way that the material rocks are made from is constantly moved around and changed   **80–81, 146, 160–161**

**rusting:** the corrosion of *iron* (or steel) as it joins with *oxygen* in damp *air* to form iron oxide   **72, 90–91, 150–151**

# S

**salt:** a *compound* produced when an *acid* reacts with a *metal* or with an *alkali*; common salt, *sodium chloride* is just one example   **65, 69–71, 129, 155, 163**

**sedimentary:** rocks made from small bits which settle in layers on the bottoms of lakes or seas   **78, 144–145, 160–161**

**slaked lime:** the chemical *compound, calcium hydroxide*   **87, 154**

**smelting:** the process of getting a *metal* from its *ore*   **149, 162**

**sodium:** a *metal element* that is soft and very reactive   **38, 53**